The
Rat

An Owner's Guide To

A HAPPY HEALTHY PET

Howell Book House

Howell Book House
A Simon & Schuster Macmillan Company
1633 Broadway
New York, NY 10019

Macmillan Publishing books may be purchased for business or sales promotional use.
For information please write: Special Markets Department, Macmillan Publishing
USA, 1633 Broadway, New York, NY 10019.

Library of Congress Cataloging-in-Publication Data
Cardinal, Ginger.
The rat / Ginger Cardinal
p.   cm—(An owner's guide to a happy healthy pet)

ISBN 0-87605-428-9

1. Rats as pets.   I. Title.   II. Series.
SF459.R3C37   1997
636.9'352—dc21   97-25735
                           CIP

Manufactured in the United States of America
10 9 8 7 6 5 4 3 2 1

Series Director: Amanda Pisani
Assistant Director: Jennifer Liberts
Book Design: Michele Laseau
Cover Design: Iris Jeromnimon
Illustration: Marvin Van Tiem
Photography:
    Front cover photo by Renée Stockdale and back cover photo by Ginger Cardinal
    Joan Balzarini: 29, 42, 82, 84, 98, 118
    Ginger Cardinal: 2–3, 26, 27, 30, 31, 33, 35, 36, 37, 38, 39, 41, 48, 60–61, 115, 120
    Photofest: 11
    David Schilling: 9, 46, 71, 74, 87, 100–101, 102, 104
    Renée Stockdale: title page, 5, 6, 13, 15, 16, 18, 20, 21, 22, 24, 43, 49, 51, 56, 58, 62,
    64, 65, 68, 69, 70, 75, 76, 77, 78, 83, 93, 94, 103, 106, 108, 109, 111, 112, 113,
    114, 122
    B. Everett Webb: 44, 54

Production Team: Chris Van Camp, Stephanie Hammett, Clint Lahnen,
Dennis Sheehan, Terri Sheehan, Karen Teo

Contents

Welcome

to the

World

of the

Rat

External Features of the Rat

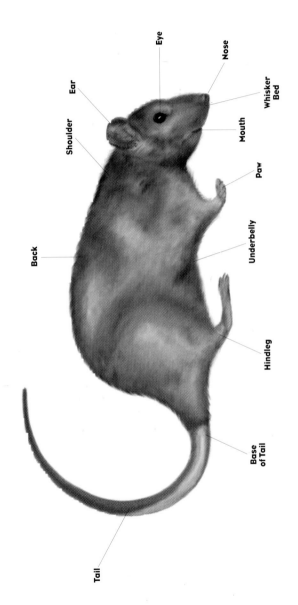

Eye

Nose

Whisker Bed

Mouth

Ear

Shoulder

Paw

Back

Underbelly

Hindleg

Base of Tail

Tail

chapter 1

The **History** of the **Rat**

Rats are delightful creatures that are often misunderstood. For many people, the word "rat" invokes images ranging from giant sewer mutants to beady-eyed, mean-spirited baby-biters. People love to hate the rat, and the reasons for this are varied and vague. One theory is that looking at a rat's eyes gives the impression of intelligence and conscious thought, which makes people feel uncomfortable. For  centuries, rats have outsmarted people trying to get the better of these rodents with traps, poisons and ratproof areas.

Rats, however, are docile animals that put eating and socializing high on their priority list. They are affectionate, loyal, social and very clean. They are quite personable and enjoy being handled. They make wonderful pets for adults and children alike.

The Rat in the Animal World

Rats belong to the order, *Rodentia*, which is the largest mammalian order. Animals in this order are characterized by front teeth adapted for gnawing and cheek teeth adapted for chewing. There are approximately 1,800 species of rodents in seventy genera and eight families. These include kangaroo rats, wood rats, hamsters and gerbils. Most rodents that are called rats have a long body, pointed nose and a long sparsely-haired or hairless tail. Rats are much larger than mice and belong to the genus *Rattus,* which contains 137 to 570 species, depending on the classification order used. For our purposes, we'll deal with two species of rat: the Black Rat *(Rattus rattus)* and the Norway Rat *(Rattus norvegicus).*

For many centuries, rats have foiled human attempts to eliminate them.

THE BLACK RAT

The Black Rat is also called the Roof Rat, Alexandrine Rat, Climbing Rat and Gray Rat. The Black Rat ranges from 6 to 8 inches in length, and its tail is just a bit longer than the body plus the head. It is dark gray-black or gray-brown and sometimes has white or lighter areas underneath. While rats are omnivorous (eating plant and animal matter) and will eat almost anything, Black Rats tend to favor plant matter. Black Rats are great climbers and jumpers. The Black Rat is believed to originally have come from southern Asia. Tests from bones have dated the Black Rat in Europe to about the fourth century, although documentation exists only from the 1200s.

Rats are believed to have been transported between the countries and continents on ships carrying exports of food and textiles. In Europe, rats quickly earned a poor reputation due to their destructive nature. Because of their great ability to jump, climb, gnaw and burrow, they have been able to stow away in places that other animals find inaccessible. Many of the exported items were contaminated or destroyed when the ship reached its destination. Illnesses were often blamed on the rat stowaways as rat droppings were seen more often than the rats. Even today, large ships take precautions against rats crawling on board from the docks.

Black Rats are not very common today. For a period in the 1800s, people speculated that they had become extinct. There are still some colonies in existence, however, in sparsely populated areas and tropical regions. It is believed, even today, that Black Rats may have carried and transmitted more than twenty diseases including bubonic plague, rabies and typhus. Their reputation for being "dirty" animals that carry diseases far precedes them. There have been many events in history where the rat was to blame for troubles with people's health, livestock, farming mishaps and lost revenue. But, by far, the single most damaging event to the rat's reputation was the plague.

The Black Rat and the Bubonic Plague

The bubonic plague was Europe's most devastating epidemic. Also called the "black death," the plague killed more than twenty-five million people, approximately one-fourth of Europe's entire population in the 1300s. The plague was transmitted via rats who were riddled with infected fleas. Because of the fleas' unusual digestive system, some of their stomach contents were regurgitated and mixed with the host's blood when they bit to feed. Therefore, when an infected flea bit a Black Rat, the rat became infected with the plague. Likewise, when an infected rat was bitten by a noninfected flea, that flea became a plague carrier. While the flea was the true carrier of the plague, the rat host was the fleas' primary means of transportation. Due to the Black Rat's transient nature—stowing away on ships and wagons—the plague spread rapidly and without mercy throughout Europe and into the Middle East, China, Turkey, Egypt, Greece, Russia, North America, South America and southern Africa. It left devastating effects in its wake, and war was waged on the Black Rat.

The plague ceased in Europe during the eighteenth century, although it continued in other countries. No one is sure why exactly, but it is speculated that rat extermination and increased sanitation requirements may have contributed to the end of the plague. There is also speculation that a large number of plague cases may have been other diseases, such as small pox, for which there was no treatment at the time. In any case, a small number of plague cases still arise today. Improved sanitation and the addition of antibiotics, such as tetracycline, streptomycin and sulfonamides, have significantly improved treatment and reduced the death rate.

THE NORWAY RAT

The Norway Rat is also called the Brown Rat, Barn Rat, Wharf Rat and Sewer Rat. The Norway Rat grows to approximately 8 to 10 inches in length, not including a 7- to 8-inch tail. The tail is approximately the length of the rat's body plus half the length of his head. This type of rat weighs 7 to 17 ounces. The Norway Rat's fur is coarser than the Black Rat's and is usually brown with lighter underparts, although wild varieties can be gray, white, black and have white markings.

The Norway Rat appeared much later than the Black Rat. Norway Rats didn't arrive in Europe until the mid-1500s and in North America until 1775. Unfortunately, the arrival of the Norway Rat was quite upsetting to the Black Rat. The Norway Rat is more aggressive and more adaptable than its cousin. Also, whereas the Black Rat tends to live in high places such as trees, roofs and attics, the Norway Rat lived in lower levels, such as basements, where food and water are more plentiful. While the Black Rat is more affected by climates and food supplies, the Norway Rat is hardly affected by temperature changes and, while it is also omnivorous and will eat almost anything, prefers animal matter. For example, Norway Rats are much more inclined to catch fish, attack poultry and feed on mice or baby livestock.

In addition to the climbing and gnawing skills of their cousins, Norway Rats also make complicated burrows and swim and dive adeptly. Although they prefer not to go in the water, they are excellent swimmers and can hold their breath for two to three minutes if necessary. Because of their adaptability, the larger and more aggressive Norway Rat quickly drove away the more "fragile" Black Rat, forcing it into areas that the Norway Rats didn't care for. For example, in the same apartment house, the Black Rats may live in the dryer and warmer attic and upper floors, while the Norway Rats would occupy the cooler and damper basement and lower floors.

The Rat Pack

In the wild, Norway Rats live in colonies of fifty to sixty rats that are often closely related. This rat pack is essential to the rat's survival. Rats gain company, socialization and support from the colony. The rat pack is one reason why poisons do not work well on a group of rats. Often one rat of the group will be designated as a taste-tester. If, after tasting, the rat doesn't get sick, the rest of the pack feels free to eat the new item. Another reason for poison's failure, of course, is the rat's great ability to adapt, adjusting to any new poisons created. Because rats are naturally cautious of unfamiliar things, they are not quick to eat anything they haven't had before, or investigate an item that is unfamiliar, such as a trap. They are also highly intelligent and able to learn from their own mistakes and the observed experiences of other rats.

Like people, rats are highly social animals.

When breeding, the rat pack helps with raising the babies. For example, when a mother is sick, injured or killed, another mother will step in and raise and feed the litter. If several rats are in a group, it is common for the babies to be cared for by multiple "mothers" even if they are not nursing. They will help clean, discipline and give affection to all the pack's babies. Most people don't realize how social these little creatures are.

Rat Legends and Myths

There are several legends and myths surrounding rats. Rats have been blamed for biting babies, spreading diseases, eating people alive, overrunning areas, driving humans out, wiping out crops and livestock, breaking into cemeteries and feasting on graves and leaping for people's throats. While, honestly, there is probably some truth to these tales, they are not the norm. It is not improbable that babies have been bitten (after all, they smell so delicious and milk-flavored), and some people who have been bitten might have thought they were being eaten alive. Rats have contributed to spreading some diseases and have had devastating effects on crops and livestock. It's true that rats have tunneled into graves and done damage, and they have had population explosions that have driven people to seek higher areas to live. As for leaping for people's throats, it is a known fact that rats have poor eyesight. In fact, most rodents have poor eyesight. Therefore, when cornered, a likely means of escape is the shoulder area next to the head which, to the rat, gives the impression of open space. So, the little rat is trying to escape toward the "open space," and is not, in fact, leaping for a person's throat. So, while there is

---

THE PIED PIPER OF HAMELIN

One of the more famous tales is the one of the Pied Piper of Hamelin. There is almost certainly some truth in this story, although the majority of it is presumed folklore. In the story, the Pied Piper promises to rid a town overrun with rats with his talented flute playing. As we now know, rats respond to high pitched squeals and squeaks. So, it's plausible that the piper did achieve a pitch on his pipe that enticed the rats to follow him. If the town was truly overrun, any number of rats following a man (odd enough in itself) would have seemed like hoards to anyone. While it's probably not plausible that the rats drowned, it is possible that a good portion was enticed into the river and carried a significant distance downstream.

some truth behind these tales, the rat doesn't deserve such a nasty reputation.

RATS IN THE MEDIA

Rats have been popular in films and books. Who will ever forget Willard and the infamous song "Ben"? Although the song sings the praises of the rats, viewers of the film just remember the oddball guy and his weird little rat friends. Of course, we all know James Cagney's famous "You dirty rat" declaration. *The Secret of NIMH*, an animated film based on the children's book *Mrs. Frisby and the Rats of NIMH*, tells the story of wild rats and mice caught by humans and given serum as lab experiments. The serum injected in these rats and mice caused their intelligence to advance radically, and they became aware of the world and its possibilities. These rats (and two mice) escaped soon after gaining this awareness and

Charming, intelligent rats are the main characters in Disney's The Secret of NIMH.

set up a rather elaborate home in a farmer's yard. NIMH, the National Institute of Mental Health, suspects that some rats have escaped with higher intelligence, and are searching the farmer's area. The rats, meanwhile, are aware of this and plan to move. Mrs. Brisby (the name in the movie) is the widow of one of the mice that escaped with the rats. She seeks the rats' help in moving her home and her sick child. It is a cute movie that gives much credit to the intelligence of rats.

Another famous rat is Ratty from *The Wind in the Willows*, friends with Toad of Toad Hall. Intelligent Ratty is forever bailing out his impulsive friend Toad. He appears in the children's books as well as in the television versions. Another literary rat is Templeton from *Charlotte's Web*, the animated film based on the classic children's book. Templeton is delightfully disagreeable as the grumbling errand boy for Charlotte. Templeton's main goals throughout the movie center around what yummy items he can get in his stomach!

Movies and television shows will utilize a rat appearance just to give people the willies or create an uneasy mood. In the Indiana Jones movies, for example, there are some scenes in which underground areas are overrun with agouti rats. The characters scream and make faces as they try to wade through the sea of rodents. Many times in film when some character is in a sewer, attic or the like, a little ratty saunters by. Of course, if you look really close, you'll notice that the rat is usually not comfortable wherever it's been placed (the side of a rushing underground stream for example) and is usually not in any big hurry to move until he figures out where he is and how to leave. Most likely, the rat will not be interested in the actor or the crew.

Often, the rat handler (the person who takes care of the rat for films) will pick a wild rat color (agouti), put a little oil in his fur to make it stand up and shine a light into his eyes to make him squint. They thereby created the mean-looking wild rat, sinisterly thinking how to get our movie hero. Usually, however, the rat is probably thinking "what is this stuff on me and who is shining that obnoxious light in my eyes?" But, to the movie industry's credit—it works. People see the rat and go "Eeeeewwww." Our little ratties definitely have public relations troubles.

Rats' Contributions

Rats have played important roles in many of the twentieth century's most important developments.

RATS IN RESEARCH

Around the early 1900s, rats and mice started being used for research. They make excellent laboratory animals due to their small size, quick reproduction and small feed requirements. The initial studies concerned diet, focusing on vitamins and minerals. Scientists were able to discover and document certain illnesses and conditions directly related to a vitamin or mineral deficiency. Rats proved to be ideal subjects because their reactions to drugs, diet changes and diseases are similar to that of humans. Rats also proved wonderful subjects for behavioral studies. They were also discovered to have a tendency to develop tumors as humans do.

Rats are useful in studying human diseases because they are similar to people in physiological and social ways.

Although no one likes the thought of harming animals unnecessarily, great advances have been made due to the study of these creatures. Cancer and allergy research have made great strides through rat research. Rats have also been used in psychological studies regarding stress, separation anxiety, aggression and habits. They've been instrumental in drug therapy for not only psychological illnesses, but also for viruses and common bacterial infections. The common cold continues to be studied using rat models.

Rats have also been instrumental in the study of heredity. In addition to the information on genetics and how traits are passed from one generation to another, scientists have been able to isolate and study the genes that cause birth defects. For centuries, people thought that certain families were cursed by insanity or punishment by the devil. Their children were born generation after generation with the same affliction.

Sometimes, these family curses would appear to be gone for a generation or two and then suddenly, as mysteriously as they had vanished, reoccur. After studying the traits passed down by rats, not only illness and birth defects, but also color and marking, scientists were able to understand the relationship between dominant and recessive genes. For example, some illnesses, like hemophilia, are linked to gender. It was discovered that the females are the carriers, which means they carry the disease in their bodies, but never actually get it. The males actually get the disease. By being able to study this and other similar diseases, scientists were able to understand how the disease is transmitted, which then enabled them to discover a treatment and, hopefully someday, a cure. By utilizing rats, who can breed one hundred or more offspring a year, scientists could study several generations in a few years. In humans, a similar study would take hundreds of years. Therefore, using rats in research helps to speed the process of developing treatments and cures.

SPACE RATS

Rats have been used in space programs. Long before anyone actually traveled in space, our little rat friends were testing machines that simulated the conditions of a journey in space. Their reactions to gravity changes, speed and dietary needs were carefully observed and monitored. Rats also took test flights in rockets to see how they were able to adapt to the "real" thing. Lucky for the rats, they did very well on the tests, and some were even heralded as heroes. If it weren't for our little rat friends, we might never have walked on the moon.

Most lab rats are the white albino or hoodeds. Both lines are old and provide years of generational data. This helps the scientists know exactly what they're getting in their test animals so that their predictions and results will not be affected by unknown genetic factors. Were it not for our little rats giving their lives and freedom up for us, our society would not be as healthy today. This is a big sacrifice for such a little animal.

INTELLIGENCE STUDIES

Rats have amazed and astounded scientists with their high intelligence, reasoning and problem-solving skills. Intelligence studies are popular even today among top scientists as well as schoolchildren of all ages. It is quite amazing to watch a rat figure out a complex maze or learn that if he does A and B, he can get to C. Rats' thinking processes continue to be studied as they are so similar to those of humans. Rats also react like humans to music, outside stimulation and memory tests. Rats have compassion for their fellow rats: Often a rat who is paired with another that has a disability, whether it is physical or mental, will be very kind to the other rat. Usually, help is offered with food, cleaning and general care. The first rat is gentle with his movements and seems to understand that the other rat is at a disadvantage.

So, as you can see, rats have a long history on this earth. They are gentle, affectionate, clean and social with their own kind as well as with people. They are closely linked with humans, choosing to live near us and share our lifestyle. They are similar to us in nature and are extremely adaptable. They are considered the next "super-race," enduring whatever catastrophes arise and flourishing in spite of them. And as I have learned, and I hope you will, they are amazing creatures.

Many people are learning about the winning personality of the rat.

chapter 2

Rats as Pets

Rats get a bad rap from much of the world, but many people have learned that rats make wonderful pets. They are clean, quiet, affectionate, need only a small amount of space and are allowed in most forms of housing, such as apartments and condos. Commonly referred to as pocket pets, they are inexpensive to feed. Unlike larger pets, they do not require walking, bathroom breaks, outside room to run or special training. They do require attention, fresh food and water, clean and safe housing and lots of love. Rats are very social and love to interact with people. You will soon find yourself inseparable from your little ratty because she is so personable. Rats will beg for your attention to be petted, held and played with.

History of the Rat Fancy

According to rat lore, during the 1800s in England, rats were kept and bred mainly for sport. That is, rats were the game or prize for dog hunts and similar activities. It is assumed (no one really knows for sure because there are no real records) that some of the breeders began keeping a few of these rats as pets and breeding some for colors. I imagine that as the rats bred, an interesting color would occur and the breeders kept it aside because it was different.

Eventually, people began keeping "fancy" rats as pets only, and around the turn of the century, a woman named Mary Douglas, commonly referred to as the "Mother of the Rat Fancy," took on the pet rat crusade and petitioned a group of mice fanciers to be allowed to join the National Mouse Club. Specific color and marking standards were set, and shows were held that included rats as well as mice. After a few years, rat fanciers were growing sufficiently to rename the club to The National Mouse and Rat Club. This continued until around the late 1920s when Miss Douglas passed away and the fancy died out for lack of participation. The National Mouse and Rat Club reverted back to the National Mouse Club (NMC), which is still active today.

RAT FACTS

Size: 14–18 inches (including tail)

Weight: 7–16 ounces

Average Life Span: 2½ years

Age at Puberty: 6–8 weeks

Breeding Season: Any—female cycles every 4–5 days; Cycling ends at 15–18 months

Gestation Period: 21–30 days (Average 21)

Litter Size: 2–24 (Average 8–12)

Weaning Age: 3–5 weeks

Housing: 10-gallon aquarium size minimum, water bottle, bedding, ventilation

Food: Rat and mouse chow, fresh vegetables and fruits

Social Needs: Rats are social creatures; keep in pairs if not able to give a lot of attention

---

Around the mid-1970s, the fanciers got renewed interest in rats and the National Fancy Rat Society (NFRS) was formed. Revised standards were established based upon known genetic keys, meetings and shows were held and a newsletter was distributed. Most rat clubs of today were fashioned in some way after the NFRS. Today there are rat clubs in most countries including Sweden, Australia, Norway and Finland, and some have more than one club. The first club in the United States, the Mouse and Rat Breeders Association (MRBA), was created around 1978. Now there are at least five or six major club entities, some of which have multiple chapters throughout the U.S.

Is a Rat Right for Me?

Rats are social creatures that thrive on company.

There are many things to consider before deciding to own any type of pet, and a rat is no exception. Before taking on such a commitment, you need to ask yourself some very important questions about your lifestyle and daily routine, and you need to give yourself some honest answers. Will I be able to spend some time each day with my rat? Will I be able to care for her basic needs and make arrangements in the event that I can't? Rats are very social creatures and thrive on company. If your schedule limits your time each day for attention to your rat, consider getting two so that they'll have company in your absence.

RAT RESPONSIBILITIES

You'll want to consider the following issues before acquiring your pet:

Does your schedule allow for time each day to spend with your rat? Will you have free time to cuddle your rat, let her out for some exercise and let your pet spend time visiting with you?

Are you willing to commit to caring for your rat's basic nutritional needs? Rats need fresh food and fresh water each day, and they thrive on fresh vegetables and grains. Will you be able to give your rat the good nutrition she needs?

Are you willing and able to keep a clean house for your rat? A rat's cage needs to be cleaned approximately once a week. This includes putting in fresh bedding and washing the cage, dishes and water bottle. Will you be able to include this in your weekly schedule of chores?

Do you have a place for your rat? Will your housing arrangements allow for a small pet, and do you have room in your home? Because rats are very social, they love to be where the action is. Will you be able to make a place in the family area so your rat can be included?

If and when you travel, will you be willing to take your rat with you? If not, can you make arrangements for someone to give your rat good care in your absence? Good care includes quality time and attention because your little rat will miss you.

Do you have children that will be handling the rat? If so, are they old enough to understand that these are small, delicate creatures that deserve the utmost care and respect when handling? Will you be able to supervise when your children are playing with the rat? Rats love kids and are very tolerant with playtime. However, they are small and can be easily injured or lost. If your children are young, it's important that you watch them closely to be sure that they don't make improper judgments.

Do you have other animals that will be interested in the rat? Dogs and cats are very interested in rats and will sometimes chase and snap at them, but they can also become the best of friends. Birds may be frightened of them (rats eat birds and eggs in the wild). Most other small animals, such as hamsters, mice and guinea pigs, simply ignore rats. Snakes are not a compatible pet for obvious reasons. Be sure to consider how your other pets may react to the rat and consider any safety concerns. We all want harmony in our households.

Will you be able to make adjustments to allow your rat out-of-cage time in your home?   Rats are notorious chewers. A rat's teeth grow continuously throughout her life, which means that your ratty must constantly keep them worn down by chewing on lots of things. In addition to electrical cords, fabric (i.e. your couch, curtains, bedspreads) and wood items, rats will shred papers (whether important or not) and gather items to hoard behind throw pillows or other "secret" places. Besides chewing concerns,

Rats enjoy digging in nontoxic houseplants like aloe vera.

you must also be aware of any houseplants that could be poisonous to your rat. Rats love foliage and will dig around in flower pots and eat the leaves and flowers. You must ratproof the area your rat will be allowed to explore.

Will you be able to commit to your pet as a member of your family?   Will you love her, care for her and keep her safe from harm? Will you provide quality food and housing and spend the money on vet bills should she become ill?

Rats as House Pets

It is too bad that rats are low on the public opinion list for rats. They are the most affectionate out of all the pocket pets. They are more sociable than hamsters, easier to hang onto than mice, more adaptable and calmer than gerbils, not as noisy as guinea pigs and much more cuddly than a goldfish. You can house them together, and they are easy to keep in most home environments.

If your rat is to be the family pet, it is important for the family to make the decision about bringing the pet into the home. Include everyone's input on preferences for color or markings, gender and any other factors. If you'll be getting two rats to keep each other company and you have two children, consider letting them each select a type of rat, but insist that they will both be family rats. This helps to give each child the privilege of picking out a baby, but doesn't create as many "ownership" problems. Nothing is more difficult to break than cries of "He's holding my rat and won't give it back!" or "Mine's too wiggly" or "I want to hold hers."

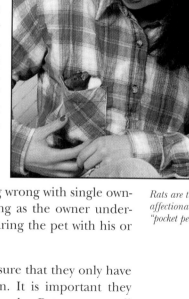

If your pet is to belong to one child and there are siblings involved, be sure they understand the concept of sharing. If the child who owns the rat isn't willing to share time with her, the other siblings may grab at the rat or take her out when no one is paying attention. This can cause accidents and injuries that can be painful and evenly deadly to your little rat. There is nothing wrong with single ownership within the family as long as the owner understands the responsibility of sharing the pet with his or her siblings.

Rats are the most affectionate "pocket pet."

If you have small children, be sure that they only have the rats out under supervision. It is important they understand how delicate rats can be. Rats are so small and cuddly that tight grips and firm hugs are often a bit too much for them. Talk with your children about how small the rat is and how gentle they must be. Even very young children can understand this

21

idea. Establish rules for handling the rat that everyone can follow. Some simple rules that can help are:

1. **Children must ask Mom or Dad before taking the rat out.** This ensures that a parent knows the rat is coming out and can supervise the playtime.

2. **Children must be sitting on the couch, chair or other specific place with the rat.** This limits the area that the rat has to run around. When there is a larger area and the rat moves fast, the child can get excited and try to grab the rat to keep her in view. Remember that rats can get up and down from furniture; your "confined space" will depend on your rat's wandering characteristics.

3. **Children cannot walk around with the rat.** This rule will prevent falls and drops. Rats can be wiggly, and when children are startled by something they're holding, they let go. For older children who you feel can walk with the rat, be sure that they do this on a carpeted area where a fall would not be so traumatic for the rat as a fall on linoleum, tile or concrete.

Make sure your children know that the other pets in the house can't play with the rat. Some pets, like this cat, would happily sample the rat as a tasty hors d'oeuvre!

4. **Do not take the rat outside.** This rule speaks for itself. There are a lot of predators outside, and it is easy for your rat to get lost if let out.

5. **Do not allow children to take the rat to their bedrooms.** This keeps your children from making poor decisions about the types of games they can

play with the rat. Keeping them in the main part of the house enables you to keep an eye on them.

6. **Do not allow children to put the rat inside anything and close the lid.** You would be amazed at how many kids don't understand the concept of oxygen. From toy boxes to lunch boxes, any type of closed area should be pointed out as a no-no.

7. **Do not allow children to make the rat hide.** Hiding can be just as dangerous as being put in a box.

8. **Make sure that children don't sit on the rat.** It's amazing how sitting on things seems to make sense when you're small. Children often sit on their stuffed animals, and rats seem to be in this same category for some. As silly as it sounds, it should be addressed.

9. **Do not let the dog or cat play with the rat.** Although some dogs and cats won't bother your rat, there are others who would be happy to sample the rat as a treat. Unfortunately, your dog or cat may act perfectly well behaved in front of you and be quite different in front of your child. Explain to them that this rule applies to all dogs and cats, so they don't try out the neighbor's dog instead.

RAT ESSENTIALS

Some good rules to remember:

To Keep Your Rat Alive:
- Clean housing
- Daily food consisting of a well-balanced diet
- Daily water

To Help Your Rat Thrive:
- Love
- Affection
- Exercise
- Playtime

---

10. **Make sure that children do not put the rat on the floor.** This is just an all-around good idea. It will help keep the rat from getting lost, stepped on, injured and accidentally let outside.

These general rules can be helpful in ways you could not foresee. I speak from personal experience when I say that even when you think you have all your safety issues covered, children will surprise you with their logic. Children don't understand a rat's limits and needs as well as adults do.

Rats and Your Lifestyle

VACATIONS

A quick word on vacations and company visiting: When you take a vacation, it is quite possible to take your ratty along. Rats love traveling with you and are easy to care for. They will adapt easily to a transport carrier for a few days and are seldom turned down at motels, the way dogs and larger animals can be. If the vacation you're taking won't be stressful on your pet for other reasons, like a very hot or cold climate, and you're not going to grandma's house where she breeds rat terriers, traveling with your rat should be no trouble.

Plan ahead for all your rat's needs, and she will love accompanying you on vacation.

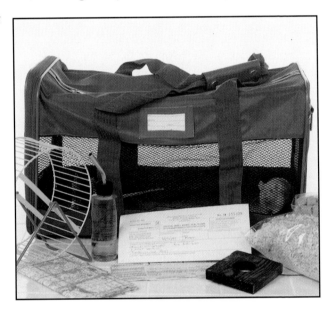

If you need to leave your rat, she will miss you. So, if you are able, the best alternative is to place her at a friend's house who understands how important your pet is to you. Make sure your friend is aware of your rat's needs as well as any social things your rat might like to do. Be aware of possible hazards, like dogs and cats, and make sure that the cage you send is escape-resistant. Your rat will do fine if she is in an environment where someone will take good care of her. And she will wait patiently for you to return.

VISITORS

When company comes, be sure they understand proper rat handling techniques. The same general guidelines should apply with company—adults and children—as in your regular household. If your company will be staying with you, make sure that they are not uncomfortable with your rat. Some people are truly afraid of small creatures, especially some older generations who have dealt with sparse times and wild rat infestations. Most people have come around to the little rat in recent years, and problems are few and far between. If, however, your company is not receptive to your pet, move your rat to a location that will be acceptable to you and your guest. Your rat will be uncomfortable with someone who jumps whenever she moves, and your company will be nervous as well. Assure your guest that your rat cannot get out. And, be sure you give your rat extra attention in her temporary place to help her adjust and not feel left out. Above all, don't let anyone tease your guest with your rat. Not only is this not funny, it can be frightening to the rat as well as to the guest, and does nothing to better public relations. Often, people who are afraid lose their fear when they are exposed to a domestic rat. Don't count on this and bring your rat out without your guest knowing, but it doesn't hurt to ask if they'd like to meet your pet. Just respect their wishes either way, and you will convince them that you are a responsible pet owner and not just keeping a rat for the novelty.

If you've taken all the precautions and considered all the factors for pet ownership, it's time to select your pet rat. The choices are varied and the selection may be difficult. Take your time and get the perfect rat for you and your family. Often, you may not be selecting your rat, she may be selecting you. Being an informed pet owner and making a logical selection will reward you with a happy relationship with your rat.

If, after considering all these things, you believe you are ready to become a rat owner, congratulations! You won't be sorry. Rats are as devoted as dogs, and you will instantly have a best friend.

3

Rat
Varieties

Rats come in all sorts of colors and markings. There are several recognized by different clubs, although there is no national standard of perfection in the United States at this time. Some people have been working toward a national standard for the fancy in the United States, and different club standards are currently being reviewed by a committee formed from members of some west coast clubs. Nevertheless, a lot of the colors were modeled after, adapted to and traded with Great Britain's National Fancy Rat Society. This society started the rat fancy in the early 1900s, and the majority of colors and markings it recognizes are based on genetics.

The following list of coat types, colors and markings is based upon a general compilation of accepted colors and my own experience.

Most of the names are common between the clubs. If there is a difference between clubs, alternate names are stated. Because there are different opinions within each club as to the color's hue, origin, cast and other specifics, all information here is written from the author's perspective, based on years of breeding, showing and judging. Opinions will vary, however, as to what is a "good" color and what class your rat would go into. If you intend to show your rat, please check with the organization's show secretary to be sure your rat is entered correctly.

Conformation

Before we discuss the colors and varieties, it is important to give an overview of the preferred rat body type. Rats should be long and racy looking with heads that are triangular, but not too pointed. Coats should be shiny with hair evenly distributed. Eyes should be round, prominent, good-sized and clear. The ears should be large, round and evenly spaced. Tails should be as long as the body plus about half the length of the head, larger at the base and tapering to a point. The ears and tail should be covered with fine hair. Males will be somewhat larger and have coarser coats and bigger builds.

This English Blue Self doe won Best in Show in 1994.

Creating a Standard

Before a rat color or marking can be shown or bred for, it must be able to "breed true"; this is to ensure that it is not just an anomaly. When a breeder creates something different, he or she has to decide if it is

27

different enough from other colors or markings to be able to have its own name.

Suppose, for example, that a breeder is working with white rats and a pink baby turns up in one of the litters (this is just hypothetical—there is no pink). The breeder really likes this color and thinks, "Wouldn't it be neat to get more pink rats?" Through selective breeding, the breeder tries to make more pink babies. Sometimes this works and sometimes it doesn't. Sometimes a color or marking you like just doesn't reoccur. But, in this case, suppose that the breeder gets pinker and pinker rats with each breeding. When the breeder decides that she has a nicely pink rat, she takes it to a club show and shows it in the Unstandardized category, which allows the judge and other breeders to see it. The judge records that this is a new color and helps decide whether it is different enough to be its own color. This is necessary to keep from breeding simple variations on a current color such as a lighter black instead of the standard black. If the new color is different enough—and our pink rat would probably be—the breeder must breed at least three different generations—the first shown pink rat, his son and his grandson—and show them at three different shows in the Unstandardized category. If these generations prove that this pink color can breed more pink rats, a standard is written and the color is voted in by the club as a new color and, usually, the original breeder gets to name it. It is then added to the club's standard and may be shown in the regular classes. It can take several years from that first pink baby to having a standard voted in.

As you can see, it isn't easy to get a new color. Some clubs, like the British club, base their colors and markings on genetic strings. If a color can't be matched up to the genetic keys, it doesn't get included in the standard. Most clubs, in the United States and in England, only vote in physical characteristics that can be proven to breed in all relevant combinations. For example, our pink rat should be able to have that color breed solid as well as all the marked varieties. However, there are exceptions where some colors occur in certain combinations.

It is assumed for this book's purpose that all coat types occur in all standardized colors and markings, all colors occur in all markings and all markings occur in all colors.

Coat Types

There are currently five standardized coat types, commonly referred to as varieties. These are hairless, rex, satin, standard and tailless. The standard coat is the original variety with the hairless, tailless and satin being fairly recent additions not recognized by all fancy clubs.

Hairless rats are more sensitive to heat, cold and other environmental conditions than their furry cousins.

Hairless   Hairless rats were created initially by breeding rex to rex. This breeding would cause the hair to be sparse or missing in some places. By selective breeding, breeders were able to create a completely hairless rat. Sometimes hairless rats have curly or wavy whiskers. Like hairless dogs, they have less chance of aggravating allergies in sensitive people; however, because of their bare skin, they are not always as willing to be cuddled as their furred friends. This may be because their skin can be very sensitive to heat, cold and other factors. These little guys need to be kept

29

especially warm and may also be more prone to skin
injuries like scratches and afflictions such as warts.

Rex   The rex rat has a curly coat. It can range from a
long coat that has some waves to a short coat with tight
curls. These rats have a reduced number of guard
hairs, which are also wavy. General preference is for
the curliest coat, however, some clubs have separate
classes for the long-coated rats. The females tend to
have the longer, wavier coats while the males tend to
have shorter, curlier ones. In all cases, whether the coat
has much curl or not, the whiskers will curl or wave.

*Rex rats have
curly coats.
(Agouti Solid
Rex)*

Satin   A satin coat is shinier than other coats. Satin-
coated rats are not standardized in all the clubs, however, because to the best of this author's knowledge,
they do not come in all colors and markings, and there
is some speculation on how shiny the coats need to be
to be considered a satin. Some rats have shiny coats
simply because they're healthy.

Standard   The original and most common coat type,
this is the standard short coat of the rat. It should be
shiny and evenly distributed with no bare spots. It
should lay flat on the rat's body with no waviness or
curliness. Any bare spots should be addressed as a
health concern.

Tailless   Tailless rats were created initially through breeding rats with unusually short tails. They are not terribly common. Because rats respire heat through their tails, tailless rats can overheat quite easily. If you have a tailless rat, or are considering getting one, you should be particularly careful if you live in a warm climate.

Tailless rats are more likely to thrive in a cool climate.

Colors

The colors of rats are divided into groups. These are solid or self, AOC (any other color) or ticked, marked, AOCP (any other color patterned) or shaded, silvered and odd-eye. Some rats fall into different classifications depending on which club you are working with. Similar colors can be in different groups within the different clubs.

SOLID OR SELF

These are rats that are a solid color throughout their whole body. There should be no white markings or white feet. There should also not be any silver or white hairs mixed in, and the coat color should be one color from the base of the hair (by the skin) all the way to the tip. Colors for solid or self rats are as follows:

Beige   This common color is a pure, warm, medium beige without gray tones or white or silver hairs. The feet and ears match the coat color, and the eyes can be either black or ruby (dark red). Sometimes the animals are separated into different classes depending on eye color: B.E. Beige (black-eyed beige) or R.E. Beige (red-eyed or ruby-eyed beige).

Black   This color should be a pure, solid black without any browning, light patches or white or silver hairs. Black should be as dark as possible. The feet and ears should be black and as dark as possible also. On exceptionally well-colored rats, even the toenails are black. The eyes are also black.

Blue or English Blue   This color is a cool medium to dark gray with a distinctive blue cast, slate-gray. The color should be even without brown spots or white or silver hairs. This color was brought over to the U.S. from the British club a few years ago. The feet and ears should be gray-blue to match the top coat, and the eyes should be black.

Champagne   This color is a pure, warm, light beige color without gray tones or white or silver hairs. It is quite a bit lighter than beige and can range from a pinkish-beige color to a light cream. The feet and ears should be the same as the coat color, and the eyes should be pink. If the eyes are darker, it is simply a Beige that is too light.

Chocolate   This color is a warm brown color resembling milk chocolate. The color should be even without lighter brown patches or white or silver hairs. The feet and ears should be chocolate color to match the top coat, and the eyes should be black. This is a difficult color to work with. Young rats often have a wonderful chocolate color, but it fades as they get older. They often get brown and black patchiness or white hairs and then resemble a poor black.

Coffee   This color is a cool light brown similar to the color of coffee with cream. The color should be even without tan patches or white or silver hairs. The feet and

ears should be pinkish-beige to light brown to match
the top coat, and the eyes should be ruby or black.

Lilac   This color is a medium gray color with a purple
cast. The color should be even without brown patches
or white or silver hairs. The feet and ears should be
light gray to match the top coat, and the eyes should be
black. This color is easily confused with the Mink or
Dove, however, the Lilac does have a purple cast to it
whereas the Mink or Dove has a brown cast.

Mink or Dove   This color is a medium grayish-brown
color resembling a mourning dove. The color should
be even without brown patches or white or silver hairs.
The feet and ears should be light gray to match the
top coat, and the eyes should be black. This color is
easily confused with the Lilac, however, the Mink or
Dove has a brown cast to it whereas the Lilac has a
purple cast.

Powder Blue Self.

Powder Blue   This color is a light blue, much lighter
than the English Blue. The color should be even, without brown patches or white or silver hairs. The feet and
ears should be light gray to match the top coat; the
eyes should be ruby.

White-Black-Eyed   This color is a pure white without yellow patches. It can range from a bright white to
a soft eggshell. Brightest white is preferred. The feet

and ears should be a pinkish-beige color, and the eyes should be black.

White–Pink-Eyed   This color is a pure bright white without yellow patches. This color is the typical "albino" with the shiny iridescent eyes. The feet and ears should be pinkish-beige, and the eyes should be pink.

White–Ruby-Eyed   This color is a pure bright white without yellow patches. The feet and ears should be pinkish-beige, and the eyes should be ruby or red. This color is easily confused with the "albino," however, they are different genetically.

AOC OR TICKED

Any other color not in the other categories. This traditionally includes "mixed" colors that have more than one color on an individual hair, or two or three different hair colors to make up the one overall color. The AOC or ticked colors are as follows:

Agouti   This color is the traditional "wild" rat color. The color should be an even muddy brown evenly mixed with black guard hairs and silver ticking. The base fur should be slate to dark gray. The belly color should be silver gray. The feet and ears should be gray-brown and the eyes black.

Amber   This color is a light orange color evenly mixed with lighter hairs. This is a paler version of the silver fawn. The base color should be cream, and the belly color should be a lighter version of the top coat. The feet and ears should be pinkish-beige and the eyes red.

Apricot   This color is a bright orange, darker than a fawn. The base color should be a light orange, and the middle of the hair to the tip is dark orange. The belly fur should be a creamy off-white. The feet and ears should be pinkish-beige, and the eyes should be ruby.

Blue Agouti   This color is an overall light to medium blue color, with each hair tipped lightly with a golden color and evenly mixed with blue guard hairs. The base of the hair is a slate blue and the belly color should be a silver blue color. The feet and ears should be blue to match the top coat, and eyes should be ruby or black.

Cinnamon or Dilute Agouti The cinnamon or dilute agouti coat is a rusty brown evenly mixed with chocolate guard hairs. It is similar to the agouti, but lighter and without silvering. The base fur should be medium gray. The belly should be light silver gray. The feet and ears should be gray-brown and the eyes black.

Cinnamon Pear This color gives the appearance of a silvery golden color. Each hair actually has three colors on it. The base color is cream, the middle color is blue and the top color of the hair is orange. There are silver guard hairs evenly dispersed. The belly color should be light silver gray. The feet and ears should be light gray, and the eyes should be black.

Fawn This color is a soft orange color. The base color should be cream, the middle of the hair is medium orange and the tip of the hair is dark orange. The belly color is creamy off-white. The feet and ears are pinkish-beige, and the eyes are ruby.

Silver Fawn.

Lynx The lynx is a cool gray-tan color evenly ticked with light chocolate guard hairs. The base of the hair should be a light slate color, and the belly color should be a light silver gray-tan to match the top coat. The feet and ears should be a light gray-beige, and the eyes should be ruby.

Pearl This is a pale creamy silver color with each hair tipped lightly with gray. The base fur should be a cream color. The belly color should be a pale silver gray. The feet and ears should be light gray, and the eyes should be black.

Pearl Self.

Red Agouti This is an even reddish brown color evenly mixed with chocolate guard hairs. It's similar to the Cinnamon with a distinctive red tone. The base fur should be medium gray. The belly color should be light silver gray. The feet and ears should be gray-brown, and the eyes should be black.

SILVERED

These rats are standardized colors that have an even mix of silver or white hairs throughout their coat. This is not to be confused with some white or silver hairs in certain spots on a solid color. This should be evenly mixed throughout the whole rat so as to give him a whole different color. The silvered colors are as follows:

Silver Agouti or Chinchilla This color is an even silver and white color evenly mixed with black guard hairs. The base fur should be medium gray. The belly color should be light silver to creamy off-white. The feet and ears should be gray, and the eyes should be black.

Silver Black   This color should be as black as possible and evenly mixed with silver or white hairs. The feet and ears should be as black as possible, and the belly color should be the same as the top coat, although a shade lighter is acceptable. The eyes should be black.

Silver Chocolate   This color should be as rich of a chocolate as possible and evenly mixed with silver or white hairs. The feet and ears should be chocolate, and the belly color should be the same as the top coat, although a shade lighter is acceptable. The eyes should be black.

Silver Fawn   This color is an orange fawn color with silver cast and evenly mixed with silver or white hairs. The base color is cream; the middle of the hair is medium orange; and the tip of the hair is dark orange. The feet and ears should be pinkish-beige, and the belly color should be a creamy off-white—not to be confused with a bright white. The eyes should be ruby.

Silver Lilac   This color should be a rich lilac color evenly mixed with silver or white hairs. The feet and ears should be gray, and the belly color should be the same as the top coat, although a shade lighter is acceptable. The eyes should be black.

Silver Mink.

Silver Mink or Silver Dove   This color should be as rich as possible, with evenly mixed silver or white hairs. The feet and ears should be gray, and the belly color should match the top coat (however, a shade lighter is acceptable). The eyes should be black.

Shaded or AOCP

These are rats that have colored points that shade into
a solid color. The colors for Siamese and Himalayan
are similar to those breeds of cats. The shaded or
AOCP colors are as follows:

Blue-Point Siamese   The color is a soft silvery blue
that gradually darkens to a medium slate blue over the
rump to the base of the tail, down the nose to the tip
and down the ankles to the feet. The tail is a medium
to dark gray color. There is not to be any white on the
body or belly. The base fur is a light slate, and the belly
color is a light silver blue. The feet and ears are
medium to dark gray to match the points, and the eyes
are red to ruby.

*A Seal-Point Sia-
mese (right) and
a Himalayan.*

Himalayan   The color is a white to off-white (as close
to white as possible) that gradually darkens to a sepia
(a dark reddish-brown) over the rump to the base of
the tail, down the nose to the tip, and down the ankles
to the feet. The tail is a medium brown color. This
color is similar to Siamese, but lighter. Points as dark of
a sepia as possible are preferred, although not easy to
achieve. The base fur is white, and the belly fur is the
same white as the top coat. The feet and ears are a
sepia, the same color as the points, and the eyes are red.

Seal-Point Siamese   The color is a medium beige
that gradually darkens to a sepia over the rump to the

base of the tail, down the nose to the tip and down the ankles to the feet. The tail is a dark sepia. There is not to be any white on the body or belly. The base fur is a cream, and the belly color is the same as the top coat. The feet and ears are sepia to match the points, and the eyes are red to ruby. This color is the original Siamese.

Markings

Marked rats come in any recognized color and have white markings that conform to one of the standardized descriptions. These rats are difficult to work with as a breeder because you have to take the color into consideration as well as the marking when selecting a nicely "showable" rat. The marked rats are as follows:

Bareback This rat has a colored hood that extends over his head to his shoulders like the Hooded, but there is no spine marking. The back and belly except for the hood are white with no spots. There is a spot on the forehead.

Chinchilla Blaze Berksire.

Berkshire This rat's top color may be in any recognized color with the underside completely white in an even line without going up onto the sides. It should look as symmetrical as possible with no brindling on the edges between the white and the color. The back feet should be white from the ankle to the feet, and the front feet should be white up half of the leg. There is also a white spot on the forehead and the tail is to be one-third to one-half white from the tip of the tail to the middle, and the middle of the tail to the rump should be the color specified by the standard color.

Blaze   This rat can be any recognized color or marking with the simple addition of a white blaze (a white area running up the center of the face). The blaze should be a wedge-shape of white that runs from the nose area to the forehead between the ears. The nose area would have the widest part with the wedge, tapering to a point between the ears.

Capped   This rat has a colored cap that only appears on the head. The color can include the ears and should extend down the side of the rat's head as if following the jaw line. There should be a spot on the forehead or small blaze between the ears where the cap meets that makes a line extending down onto the face, but it should not go past the eyes. The rest of the rat should be white.

Hooded   This rat has a colored hood that extends from his head to his shoulders and should go all the way around underneath his body so that it is solid. There should be no white markings within the hood either on top or underneath (i.e. chin). There is also a line or spine marking of the color that runs from the hood down the back and into half of the tail. The spine marking should be a nice even width, approximately $\frac{1}{2}$ to 1 inch, be as straight as possible and be solid with no breaks.

Irish

American Standard   This rat has an oval, egg-shaped white marking on his belly. The white area should be as close to an oval as possible.

English Standard   This rat has a triangular shaped white area on his chest between his two front legs. The triangle, which is inverted, should have the widest part between the front legs with the "top" point on the bottom toward the belly. The triangle should be as large and even as possible without extending onto the rat's neck or legs or down his belly.

Masked   This rat has a band of a recognized color on his face that covers the area around the eyes. It should not extend anywhere else on the face. The rest of the body is white.

VARIEGATED

American Standard   This rat has medium-sized distinct colored spots evenly disbursed along his back, sides, tail and belly.

Dalmatian   This rat has small distinct colored spots, sometimes referred to as "splashes," evenly disbursed throughout his body. The difference between the American Variegated and the Dalmatian is the size of the spots. The American Variegateds were bred first; the Dalmatians are a more recent breed.

English Standard   This rat has a colored hood that extends over his head to his shoulders like the Bareback, but then has distinct colored spots evenly disbursed along his back, sides, tail and belly. There should be a white spot on the forehead.

Lilac Blaze English Variegated.

ODD-EYE

Odd-eye rats must be a recognized color and/or marking. They are distinguished by having one dark eye and one light one. This is usually one black eye and one ruby eye, although other variations do occur. These rats are classified differently because, in addition to the eyes not following the specific standard, the different colored eyes often dilute the coat colors and make it difficult for them to compete in regular classes.

A Note on Unstandardized Rats

As mentioned previously, there is usually an Unstandardized class for rats that don't fit into a current standard, but which the breeder feels may turn out to be a new color or marking. This class is important for documentation purposes in establishing standards and is also a good learning experience for the breeder who may not know that a color he is generating is simply a mutation of something else. This is mostly a class for the breeders and is judged more casually because it is a sort of "work in progress" section. These rats may not compete with the standardized rats for Best in Show.

The Dumbo Rat is a docile, "lap rat," and is becoming more and more popular as a pet.

One type of rat that is not standardized at this time, but I feel is worthy of mentioning is commonly referred to as a "Dumbo" or "Elephant Ear" rat. These rats have ears that are a bit larger than usual and sit offset on the top one-third of the side of the rat's head. This trait gives them a distinctly passive appearance; they bear a resemblance to Fievel from the animated Disney movie *An American Tale*. These rats are very docile and are quickly gaining in popularity. In general, they are much calmer than your average rat and tend to be very sweet, mellow lap rats. Although they are difficult to come by, an increasing number of breeders are breeding Dumbo Rats, and they will become more available in the future.

chapter 4

Selecting
Your Rat

So, now that you've decided on a rat, which kind should you get? Should you go to a pet shop or a breeder? Male or female? Pedigreed? Baby or adult? Are some colors better than others? There is a lot to consider. It is much easier to think about what you want and have that in mind than it is to just go shopping at the mall and see what you find. You're making a commitment to the rat for her lifetime, and you want to be sure that you get one that will make you happy. If you're happy, you'll have a happy rat.

43

Guidelines for Acquiring Your Rat

I think it is very important for a prospective rat owner to establish and follow guidelines when choosing a rat. Unfortunately, with any animal, sometimes it's just love at first sight and that's just that. Of course, who am I to stand in the way of true love? However, it is especially sad to fall in love with an animal that has health problems and puts your heart through the wringer. Health is the most important consideration, but for now, let's assume that all rats are healthy. You need to decide what other criteria you will use to make your decision. It's good to list the qualities that you feel are important and desirable. Discuss this with the family if your rat will be a family pet so everyone provides input.

Sometimes, you will find your rat through love at first sight.

MALE OR FEMALE

Gender is a good place to start, especially because most places will keep their males and females separated. Males, as a general rule, are larger, have coarser hair, are lazier or more laid-back and more prone to skin troubles (most of which just require additional bathing or a change in diet). Females, on the other hand, tend to be smaller, friskier, more playful and more mischievous. Since nothing is absolute and each ratty has his or her own individual personality, gender assumptions may not always be borne out, but general guidelines are a good place to start. If you have small children or are looking for a rat to hang out with you and cuddle, a male might be a good idea. Males are better suited to shoulder riding and lap sitting. If you enjoy the antics of the ratties and like to play with your pets, a female might be a good choice. Females are better suited to entertainment and will delight you with their activities.

Sexing the rat is usually done by the pet shop or breeder. In some instances, however, you may need to make your own determination. The sex of a rat is pretty easy to determine by four weeks of age. The males will have a pronounced scrotum. Their testicles may not be apparent, but the sac is hard to miss. If it isn't there, it is a female (unless you're looking at a neutered male). If you're unsure, look at several rats until you find two different ones. This will certainly help you with your diagnosis.

HOW MANY? ONE, TWO, THREE?

Rats are very social. They enjoy company and can get bored or lonely. If you are going to be spending a lot of time with your rat, i.e. you work at home or plan to take your rat out with you, one may do fine. Most people, however, do well to get two rats. If possible, try to get two of the same sex while they are young; litter-mates are ideal. While some animals are more social toward people if they are solitary, this is not the case with rats. You could have six and they would still all be dying for your attention when you walked in the room. So, unless you are able to spend a lot of time with your rat, seriously consider getting a pair to keep each other company.

AGE

Most rats that are available are youngsters. The average age of babies for sale or adoption is usually between four and six weeks. These are the cutest of the bunch and can very easily sway your decision with just a twinkle in the eye and soft whiskers on your cheek. With the short life span of rats, babies are probably preferable as you will be getting the most from your time spent, and there is nothing like bonding with your baby. A teenager or adult can be just as lovable, however, and should not be ruled out if you have an opportunity. From a show standpoint, a baby's color is not definitive, as they molt several times before their true adult color comes in. Often, you can get greater satisfaction from adopting an older animal that truly needs a home. Sometimes, these older rats are very affectionate, making up for lost time when they didn't have their own person to play with.

COLOR OR MARKING

A certain color or marking doesn't affect your pet's temperament, but it can affect your ultimate satisfaction. You may love your pet to pieces and not want to trade her for the world, but that doesn't mean you don't wish you'd gotten a certain variety originally.

Rats are very social creatures who will bond both with other rats and with humans.

Where to Get Your Rat

There are many places you can get your rat. The following is a list with the advantages and disadvantages of each.

PET SHOPS

There are many pet shops in most areas and it is common for them to carry rats.

Pros:

- A pet shop may have a big variety because they acquire rats from different breeders.

- You have someplace to go back to if there's a problem and you need questions answered.

- They can watch their incoming stock for a specific color or marking that you're interested in.

- You can acquire everything in one trip—food, water bottle, cage, bedding and rat.

Cons:

- The majority of rats in pet shops are there to serve as feeders, rather than as pets, and are therefore not handled very much. Also, a lot of pet shops keep all their rats together, and if you purchase a "teenage" female, she may be bringing home a surprise for you in a couple weeks.

- The staff's focus is not usually on the small animals, therefore, you may not be able to speak to someone who knows much about rats or you may get misinformation.

- You may not like the type of food or the cage that they have.

- You may make an impulse purchase on an animal that you wouldn't ordinarily have considered due to excitement, impatience or that guilt of "saving" one.

If you make a trip to the pet shop, set some ground rules on whether you will or won't make a purchase and under what circumstances. Ask the staff if there is anyone there who is knowledgeable in rats. Ask if their particular rats have been handled or if they have pet rats. Ask if they keep their males and females separated. Some pet shops separate their "pets" from their "feeders" in an attempt to place nice rats in homes. Be careful in your selection and follow the guidelines.

BREEDERS

Some areas will have breeders that breed specific colors and markings for clubs or shows in their area.

Pros:

- A breeder may have better show-quality rats, nicer or more unusual colors.

- You have someone to call with questions who should be able to give you answers.

- If you're looking for a specific color or marking, they may be able to refer you to someone who can help you.

Cons:

- You may be limited to choose from what the breeder specializes in.

- If the breeder has many rats, some of the animals may not be well handled.

- You may feel obligated to get a rat since you took up their time.

If you want a show-quality rat, like this Silver Fawn, with more unusual colors or markings, a breeder may be your best bet.

If you make a trip to a breeder's home, be specific about what you're looking for. If you don't know, be honest. If personality is your main concern, state it and be willing to compromise on all the neat colors. Establish guidelines before you go on what conditions you will get a rat. Be careful in your selection and follow the guidelines.

NEWSPAPER AD

Most newspaper ads that feature rats are the result of "accidental" pregnancies.

Pros:

- The babies were probably handled a lot and well socialized.

- The price is usually reasonable.

Cons:

- Because the owners are not pet specialists, the rats may have illnesses or have been exposed without their knowledge.

- You may feel obligated to adopt one to help them out.

If you follow up on an ad, ask questions about where and how they got their rat, any health concerns, colors, markings and so on, so that there are no surprises if you decide to look. Establish your criteria for acquiring a rat. Be careful with your selection and follow the guidelines.

CLUB SHOWS OR MEETINGS

If you are lucky enough to live near a club that has meetings or shows, you can shop for your rat there.

Pros:

- You may get a more varied selection of show- and pet-quality ratties.

- You could get second opinions from other attendees on the health and/or cuteness of your selection.

If you adopt a rescue rat, you will be getting a wonderful pet and giving a needy animal a home.

Con:

- You can be easily overwhelmed by the number from which to choose and make a rash decision.

If you decide to shop for a rat at a club meeting or event, be sure you look at all your choices and think carefully while enjoying the other activities before you make your decision. Establish your criteria for acquiring a rat and follow the guidelines.

CLUB RESCUE GROUPS OR LOCAL SHELTERS

If you are looking to give a needy ratty a home, some clubs have rescue groups and some shelters have rodent areas.

Pros:

- You would be providing a home for a rat that would otherwise have an uncertain fate.
- You may be able to get established roommates.

Cons:

- As with any adopted animal, you don't know what the rat's background may be regarding socialization, age and so on.
- If she's a solitary animal, it may be difficult to place her with another.

Call and get all the facts before visiting any available animals. Be sure she's a good pick for you and your family because you don't want to bounce her around any more homes than necessary. Establish your criteria before going and follow the guidelines.

Making Your Choice

When you have in mind what type of rat you are looking for and you have selected a place to shop, now is the time to evaluate the actual ratties. Your first concern and evaluation should be health. Are the cages clean? Do they have food and water? Are the rats active; do they have a good weight and a shiny coat? Are they paying attention and curious about what you're doing?

EVALUATING HEALTH

If rats are showing signs of illness, symptoms can include: sneezing (almost continuous), sleepy eyes, mucous around the nose, hunched back, fur standing up, diarrhea, wheezing or rattling noises, scabs or sores with bald patches and lethargy or lack of interest. Keep in mind that some of these things, in moderation, may have other causes. For example, some rats will sneeze right after their cage is cleaned or if it is dusty or breezy, but in these cases the sneezing is not continuous and there is no sleepy-eyed look or smeared mucous. Also, some rats can get a form of diarrhea from fear or nervousness. This type of diarrhea, however, is simply soft, smelly stools. It should not be watery, and there should be no fecal matter on the rat. Diarrhea due to nervousness is usually short-lived. This is common if the rat has just traveled to a new area or been moved to a different cage, especially if she's young. These factors are exceptions, but the other items listed are highly suspect, and you probably shouldn't get a rat from that cage or that place. As usual, you need to use your own common sense and good judgment. Look for rats that are alert, active, curious and inquisitive. Check for clear, bright eyes and clean, shiny fur. Watch for good weight so you know that they've been well fed.

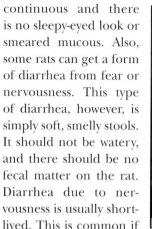

Choose a rat that is healthy, alert and active.

EVALUATING TEMPERAMENT

After you've established reasonable health, it is time to check out the babies. Look in the cage first without opening it. The babies should be curious about what you're doing, and many will climb or jump as high as they can to get close to you. They want to check you out and see what you're doing. This is a good sign of well-socialized rats. After you open the cage, let them react first. If the rats fly to the corner with their ears up and their eyes wide and the pile constantly changes to

51

see who gets stuck on top, this is not a good sign. Rats like this usually have not been handled much and are quite frightened. A rat from this bunch can be a pet, however, she will always be a bit nervous or shy and will probably not do well in unfamiliar situations. Rats like these are not really a good choice. If, however, the rats remain at the top of the cage near you or are leaping or standing up to see you, this is a plus. Some rats may fly to the corner when the cage is first opened and may venture back out cautiously to see you after the lid is off. This is generally okay as they may simply have just been moved and are still nervous in their new environment. The main thing to watch for is that the rat wants to come see you.

PLAN AHEAD

- Where in your home will you keep your rat?

- Will your family be willing to handle your rat gently?

- Will a rat make your house-guests uncomfortable?

- How will you ratproof your home?

- Will your other pets learn to live comfortably with your rat?

After talking to the rats for a few minutes, you can reach in, let them sniff you, pet them or pick one up. Be sure your hands are clean, for the rat's health and also to keep your fingers from being nibbled. The rat should not run from you when you reach for her and she shouldn't squeak, wiggle or scratch to get back down. Again, a rat like this may seem interested in you immediately after being put back down, but she is a poor choice for a pet. The ideal pet should be anxious to be picked up and should immediately begin checking YOU out. She will sniff you and rub her soft nose and whiskers on your cheek. Some rats may lick you. This is as much for your salt as it is a sign of acceptance and affection. Your heart may melt when you are kissed by a baby rat. Some rats will boldly crawl from your hand right up to your shoulder and begin fussing with your hair. Be careful putting a baby rat on your shoulder—when she's young, her attention span is short and she can fall. Now, if you haven't been sold on this little baby, you can put her back and visit another one. Be forewarned, once you pick up a baby, she will want to be picked up again; you will often find yourself trying to get around the ones you've already picked up to see the ones you haven't. It is common to have a crowd clamoring to get in your hand. They just love the attention.

Once you've chosen your rat(s), and you have all your necessary housing, food and water supplies (see chapter 5, "Housing Your Rat," for a list of necessary supplies), make sure you are able to take your new pet home safely. The most comfortable way for you and for your pet is to have a carrier for transporting. This will keep your rat safe while you're driving and keep you from being distracted. It will also keep the kids from grabbing and arguing over who gets to hold her.

Bringing Your Baby Home

When you get your baby home, she will have a lot to adjust to. She will be most comfortable if she is near you, so even if your rat's permanent home may not be in the middle of the household, try to keep her there for the first few days. She'll enjoy getting to know your house and routines and appreciate the company. When you first arrive home, place your rat into her cage and let her be by herself for a little while. She'll need to examine her new home and become familiar with her surroundings. You might notice some rearranging of the furniture or some major housecleaning going on. Rats are fastidious housekeepers and very finicky about where things are. She is making her cage her home. Since she is still a baby, it is a good idea to give her a little box or something similar for her to curl up and sleep in. This will give her a safe, secure place to be. If the kids want to watch her during these first few hours, the rat usually won't mind as long as there isn't any cage-tapping going on. Your rat will check you out and then return to her business, getting her home settled.

Handling Your Rat

When handling rats, you will find that some are more rambunctious and some are more laid-back. This is inherent in personality. Busier rats will most likely want down to explore and look around, while laid-back rats will be better suited to laps and shoulder-riding.

One item of concern when handling rats is their nails. A rat's nails can be quite sharp and may even scratch you when you hold her. This is due to her gripping you to hang on and isn't personal. Some rats' nails are sharper than others. This can be due to their activity— for example, if your rat is a great digger during house-

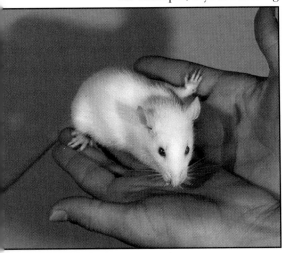

cleaning, her nails may not be too sharp. If she chooses to move things around a bit, her nails may be more pointy. If you'd like to trim her nails, this is possible and commonly done. Most people use finger-nail clippers and care must be taken to avoid the "quick," which is the area where the dead part of the nail meets the live part. You

When you handle your rat, you may find that her nails need some attention.

can usually tell this because you will see a little line of blood going across the nail at a certain point. If you have experience with trimming, you can do this regularly at your home. If you don't have experience, you may want to consult your vet, a breeder or a pet shop for instruction.

I personally don't care for clipping nails. It is necessary on some rats, but because they are so wiggly when being held for this, I worry about missing and getting a toe. For my purposes, I have found an emery board or file to be the best alternative. I simply rub the rough side back and forth along the nail tip until it is suffi-ciently smooth (it doesn't take long). This usually has to be done more often than clipping, but I feel this method is safer and I get less opposition from my rats. You'd be surprised how sharp nails can keep the fam-ily from wanting to hold your pet. This little routine maintenance can make a big difference.

Rats on the Loose

Rats love to be loose in your home. They are naturally curious and playful. They want to check every nook and cranny of your home and will do so if they can. Unfortunately, due to their small size, they could get hurt. Although you can't foresee every possible hazard, there are precautions you can take to limit the chances of your rat being lost or injured. The best idea is to limit her play area. This could be a couch, a bed or a table. If you want your rat to have room to run along the floor as well, it is best to select one room for this activity.

- Ensure that the room can be enclosed. This will help keep her safe. This is especially important if you have other pets that may want to snack on your rat.

- Rats are notorious chewers; nothing is safe. One of the biggest chewing concerns is the electrical cord or phone cord. Enclose your cords in PVC pipe then tape them to the wall, keeping them out of the way.

- Your rat may try to use corners as a bathroom or may dig in the corners and actually get up a portion of your carpet! If the room is carpeted, consider putting remnants in the corners or tacking down the material.

- Make sure there are no plants that would be poisonous to your rat. Any plant that is poisonous to a dog, cat or child could affect your rat also. Keep azaleas away from your rat. In addition to eating plants, your rat may also enjoy digging in your pots. There is nothing like the sight of soil flying in all directions to get you flying off your chair. Because digging is as instinctive as chewing, it is best to put plants out of reach when your rat is out.

- Be careful of furniture that your rat could get caught in, such as recliners. Some couches also can have a framework that enables the rat to crawl up inside. There is nothing more frustrating than not being able to reach your pet when it's time for her to go back in her house. If you suspect she is not stuck and just lounging, try tempting her with a piece of food. As a last resort, put her cage in the room and she will usually go in it eventually. If you suspect she is stuck, *don't* pull her. You could seriously injure her. Elicit the help of other family members or friends to help secure your rat's release. Rats rarely get truly stuck, so don't be surprised if after all this hoopla, your rat saunters out to see what all the commotion is.

If you let your rat run unsupervised around your house, she can get into all kinds of trouble.

- Check under your furniture and all around your walls for holes that could enable your rat to escape the room. You don't want to lose your rat because she found a hole and decided to be a great explorer. Make sure you plug up any holes that she could possibly escape through, even if you think it is too small.

- And, finally, use a sheet, blanket or throw on your furniture if you're concerned about urine marking or chewing. This will help prevent accidents and make your relationship with your rat much more harmonious.

Your rat will enjoy her time out with you and will give you many delightful hours of merriment when she has a big play area. Making it safe for her will help you both enjoy your time together.

Rats and Kids

Rats are very tolerant of children. But, because they are small creatures, they can be easily hurt. It is important to educate your children on the rat's safety and well-being. Children under the age of eight should never have the rat out unsupervised, and older children should still be monitored. Children don't often make good choices on what is "fun" for the rat. Riding your ratty in a baby buggy or dump truck is not a terrible thing if you're careful, but loading your ratty in your backpack to go for a bike ride is not a good choice. Giving her a bath may sound harmless, but it if it's in the backyard pool, it can be traumatic or even dangerous for your rat.

The best thing to do is discuss with your children the attributes of the rat, such as her small size and the fact that she depends on us for her safety. Review things that she can do and things that she shouldn't do. Make sure they understand that even a "minor" accident could seriously injure their pet. Decide on rules for having the rat out for playtime. For example, my children must have our small animals in the living area where they can be observed. They are not allowed in their bedroom without supervision. This is especially important when friends are over, as they tend to get more rambunctious with the animals.

It is also important to discuss signs that the rat is not having a good time. For example, a rat should never squeak. Rats only do so if they are frightened, hurt or fighting with another rat. Your child should know that if she squeaks, something the child is doing or has done is not comfortable for the rat. She is probably afraid, annoyed or hurt. Do let children know, however, that you understand that accidents can happen and that if one does, to come tell you immediately. There's nothing worse than finding your bleeding animal in her cage and "nobody" knows what happened to her. Rats are extremely resilient and escape most possible injuries. Most cuts, if they occur, are superficial and just require first aid. Luckily, the rat's agility does her a great service.

Rats and Other Pets

If you are bringing your rat home and there are other pets in your household, they will be naturally curious. However, it is important to distinguish curiosity from

Most dogs will learn to tolerate, and many even enjoy, the company of a pet rat.

jealousy. Make sure that your dog or cat understands that this is a new member of your household and not a special snack just for him. Most cats are not terribly interested in the rat after the initial newness wears off. They are too big to mess with. Now mice on the other hand . . . Be sure you give your other pet lots of attention. Let him observe the rat in her cage before you give him an up close and personal introduction. Fido could easily swallow your baby in one gulp if he wanted to. As a general rule, dogs and cats will usually tolerate and in some cases, even enjoy a rat's company. Rats don't always understand that they are small, and once they feel they're a member of the family, they don't mind throwing their weight around. This can mean that your cat will get kicked off your lap by your rat or your dog may lose his toys and treats to your rat's stash.

Birds, however, are not usually a good match with rats. In the wild, birds and rats are natural enemies. In survival of the biggest, rats will eat small birds and bird eggs. Large birds will prey on rats as well. So, as a general rule, most birds are nervous and even frightened around rats. Rats, however, are extremely interested in birds. They're sure they would be tasty if they could just get a nibble. You need to be careful with birds and rats. Your rat could attack and/or kill a small bird such as a parakeet or even a cockatiel. A large bird like a parrot could injure or kill your rat, and the rat may put her-self in harm's way by not having any fear of the large bird. It is best, if you have a bird, to take precautions that they will not be able to get near each other.

Rats Will Learn to Live on Schedule

Once you get your ratty settled in your home, you will find hours of enjoyment in her personality. Rats give all of themselves and truly enjoy being with you. You'll find they quickly become members of your household and will adjust their schedule according to yours. Although rats are nocturnal by nature, your rat will get up any time to play or be with you and will soon learn your routines. She will be waiting for you when you get home from work or school, looking for her personal people time. Give your rat basic care and your love and affection, and she will reward you with a lifetime of devotion.

Caring
for Your

part two

Rat

chapter 5

Housing
Your Rat

Your rat's home is very important to him. Rats like to have the comfort of their own places. It is very common, even for rats who have free rein, to have their personal spots to use for private time. Once you have decided to acquire a rat, try to set up the cage area before bringing your rat home. This will help your ratty have a comfortable place when he is introduced to his new household and will also help your family make the transition.

What You'll Need

CAGE

The cage will be your biggest investment and your rat will have it for a long time. Be sure you get a cage that will suit your preferences and your household and one that is suitable for your rat. There are many options; you can get cage recommendations from friends or store personnel. In general, you should choose a cage that is at least 24 inches long, 12 inches deep and 12 inches high. It should be gnawproof, free of sharp edges, have adequate ventilation and secure closures and doors. You'll also have to consider where to put the cage. Consider the average temperature of the area the cage will be in, how accessible and easy this area is to clean and any other factors that can affect your rat's health and safety (i.e. Will the cage be placed low enough for small children or other pets to reach it?).

Wire Cages

If you live in a warm climate, a wire cage may be a good choice for you as it gives the most air circulation. Wire cages also help to satisfy a rat's natural urge to climb, and toys may be hung to dangle from the top. When selecting a wire cage, keep a few key points in mind. The size of the wire openings must be no larger than $\frac{1}{2}$-inch square. Lots of wire cages are made for larger pets like rabbits and have larger gauge wire. This is not safe for your rat as he can sometimes escape through the openings. It is also possible for him to get a limb stuck through one of the squares. This can be highly dangerous as a rat's hind leg bends in such a shape that it is not easily maneuvered, especially by a hysterically panicking rat who is trying to get his leg unstuck. A situation like this can result in bite wounds to other rats or yourself while trying to help the terrified victim, or in bloody injuries and broken limbs.

> ### HAVE YOUR HOME READY FOR YOUR RAT
>
> Items you'll need to have on hand when you bring your new rat home include the following:
>
> • Cage
>
> • Bedding
>
> • Food dish
>
> • Water bottle
>
> • Food
>
> Items that are nice to have for your convenience and fun for your rat include the following:
>
> • Treats
>
> • Toys
>
> • Exercise equipment
>
> • Pet carrier

Wire floors should definitely be avoided for similar reasons. Cages with wire floors are most often used for

A wire cage provides better air circulation and a place for the rat to satisfy his natural urge to climb.

rabbits, whose heavily furred large feet don't have problems with this arrangement. The rat, however, does have difficulties. A rat's foot can fall in between the squares on some wire floors, which can result in injuries and broken limbs. Also, rats can get foot infections and abscesses from the constant pressure of the wire on their bare feet. Rats should be able to walk directly on their bedding. If your cage of choice has a wire floor that can be removed and a tray that can be used as the bottom, it is possible to use the cage safely. When removing the wire floor, be sure you use special cutting implements that do not leave sharp edges, or consult a metal fabricator or cage maker in your area for modifications. Also, make sure the doors and openings are secure and will not be able to be "broken into" by the family dog or cat. If the cage has a door that is spring-loaded or opens by pushing the handle in to release it, be sure you put a safety clip pinning the door to the cage to prevent accidents.

Wire cages have better airflow, which is a consideration in warmer areas. However, they also result in bigger messes due to the rat kicking shavings out of the cage each time he cleans house. If your rat is to be in a main family room in a wire cage, be sure you are willing to clean up the stray shavings regularly. Wire cages can also corrode after a few years and must be replaced.

Aquariums or Plexiglas

Aquariums are also common containers for rats. Plexiglas containers are usually used for mice and hamsters, but some are large enough for rats. Aquariums are nice because they allow you to view your pet unobstructed. There is no spillage of shavings onto the floor during ratty housecleaning, and their regular sizing makes it easy to find a suitable spot in the family home. While the Plexiglas containers usually have factory lids, most standard aquariums do not have suitable lids for small animals. There is a line of aquariums made for critters that have half-glass and half-screen mesh tops, and also one that has a screen mesh lid that slides in. If you have a standard tank, you may need to purchase an after-market top. Commercial pet companies make such tops that are plastic framed and enclosed with mesh. Some clubs have members that make similar tops that can incorporate food and water holders. Your choice will probably have to be made based on availability.

Aquariums are more enclosed than wire cages, and, therefore, air circulation must be a concern, especially if you live in a warm climate. During the summer months, it is possible, if the rat does not have adequate ventilation or cooling items in his tank, for him to develop heatstroke. You will need to add more toy items in an aquarium to satisfy your rat's urge to climb, and you will have to provide a water bottle holder to enable your rat to have fresh water at all times. Another problem with aquariums is that they are easily broken. They can be heavy and awkward to carry, especially for children. A bump in the right place during a cage cleaning and your cage could crack, break or even shatter. While shattering is not common, it can happen. You can find used aquariums at swap meets, garage sales and some pet shops. If the aquarium is in need of repair, be careful about how you do so. Tape, silicone bonding agents or hot glue on the inside can all be chewed or eaten by your rat.

Aquariums allow you to observe your rat unobstructed, and often make tidier homes for your rat.

BEDDING

Bedding is a hot issue among rat owners. Your choices used to be very limited, but in recent years with scientific studies and industry advances, there are several options for the rat owner. As a general rule, bedding should be changed frequently to keep your rat's home clean and odor-free. By nature, rats are clean animals with relatively little odor and they enjoy staying that way. Depending on the size of your cage, the number of occupants, your climate and the housecleaning personality of your rat, a cage cleaning once a week should be sufficient. Some rats may require more. You should put enough bedding in the cage to cover the bottom and a cushion of extra bedding to allow the rat to move it around. Rats like to rearrange their bedding and cage items. Some will make nests with bedding and some simply shift it to different places. Some rats are busier than others. In cooler times, extra bedding is nice for rats to make a fluffy sleeping corner.

There are several different types of bedding on the market, but not all types are readily available in all areas. Each type has its pros and cons. Try what you feel would best suit your household, what you can easily find in your area and what you can afford.

Cedar Cedar is a common form of bedding that is readily available in most pet stores and grocery or superstores. This is unfortunate because it can be very unhealthy for the rats as well as for other animals. People buy it because it smells so nice and helps to repel parasites, but these advantages don't begin to make up for the devastating effects on your rat's health. It has long been determined in lab experiments that cedar causes respiratory ailments in rodents. Rats suffering from these illnesses sneeze almost constantly and have red, dried secretions around their eyes and nose and a rattling sound in their lungs.

It was originally thought that the cedar gave off spores that were airborne and inhaled by the rat. These, in turn, embedded in the lungs and caused injury to lung tissue. This was an ongoing process by which the rat's lungs were reinjured and built up scar tissue. The subject was debated long and fiercely as to why rats would be infected with this condition, while humans living in a cedar home were not. The theory was that the cedar shavings being kicked and pushed around by the rats were constantly being broken and releasing the spores whereas cedar in a home was intact. Also, humans didn't sleep curled up on their cedar.

As years went on and more experiments were conducted and data compiled, new information came to light. The good smell of cedar is due to a chemical called phenol. This substance, to varying degrees, can be poisonous and caustic. The phenol is presumably released when the cedar gets wet either from urine or water bottle drippings. When the phenol is inhaled by the rat, it irritates the nasal passages, throat and lungs. Phenol is a toxic chemical, and it also enters the bloodstream and takes its journey through the body. The liver and kidneys, responsible for filtering toxins from the body, remove the phenols. The phenol can build up in these organs and cause eventual illness and organ failure. These conditions can also weaken the rat's system, making it ripe for other illnesses to invade. So, you can see why this bedding is a poor choice and draws much controversy. You will, inevitably, hear stories from people who kept their rats on cedar for years and never had a problem. I don't doubt it. Animals are individuals just like people, and it's possible for rats to survive, due to their revered adaptability, and thrive despite the odds against them.

Pine Pine shavings are getting bad press lately in the rat circles with the same phenols being blamed. The amount of phenols in the pine shavings, however, is significantly less than in cedar. Pine shavings also have a nice odor and because they are not colored, do not stain the coat. These are readily available in grocery stores, superstores, pet supply stores and feed stores. Several different types of animals utilize pine, from horses to rabbits. For our rat's purpose, you should get a packaged shaving that is as dry and dust-free as possible. Dusty shavings can make your ratty sneeze just as much as illness. Never place shavings that are wet in your rat's cage. Be sure to keep them in a dry area. It is also a good idea to scoop out the corner that your rat uses as his relief area daily. Shavings can vary from a hard chip to a soft curl. I prefer the soft curly one that is compressed and has relatively little dust.

Aspen   Aspen shavings are a recent addition. They are a hardwood like cedar, but supposedly do not carry the phenol chemical. They come in generic forms as well as from some commercial carriers. Unfortunately, availability is not widespread at this time, and you may not be able to find them in your area. Feed stores and larger pet supply stores are your best bet. Also, some pet shops may be able to order aspen shavings for you.

Corn Cob   Corn cob can be used for rats, but it is not very practical. It is difficult for rats to step on (it rolls and moves under their feet) and there is no absorption feature. It is thought that corn cob may contribute to drying a cage, and it is not a good choice if you live in a particularly dry climate. However, it is dust-free and may be good for some families with allergy problems.

For your rat's purposes, purchase pine shavings that are as dry and dust-free as possible.

Alternative Products   There are other commercial bedding products. Some are made from recycled paper products and some are from other natural sources such as hay. The consensus is that while most pet owners feel safer using these products, they are significantly more expensive and difficult to find. Some do not control odor well. There have also been reports of people being allergic to some products. As always, test what works best for your household and your rat.

Pictured here are some supplies you should purchase before you bring your rat home, including a cage, bedding, toys and chew blocks.

NESTING MATERIALS

Some rats love to have big nests and will try their darndest to steal what they can for them. For these guys and for others, it is helpful to offer napkins or paper towels to help with their nesting. They will love shredding them and making their home. If you have a choice, white paper is probably the best choice to avoid potential problems with dye allergies. Commercial nesting materials really aren't necessary for rats although some rats do enjoy them. Other alternatives include hay, straw or grasses.

FOOD DISH

Once you decide which type of cage to get, you can begin purchasing the accessories such as a food dish. If you have a wire cage, you have the option of a food dish that mounts directly to the wire. If you have an aquarium, or if mounted food dishes are not available in your area, you will need a weighted bowl. Ceramic crocks work well. If a dish is too light, your rat may simply dump his food out when he climbs on the edge to see what's in there. After he picks and chooses what he'd like to eat, he will go on his merry way. Later, when he's hungry again, he'll be digging and sifting through the shavings looking for the stuff he rejected the first time. This can be very wasteful, and you can never be sure how much or what he's eating, causing you to overfeed because his food bowl is always empty. There are some weighted plastic crocks on the market, but I find that rats don't have any trouble tipping these over. The ceramic crocks seem to stay upright the longest.

WATER BOTTLE

Rats must have a constant supply of fresh water. Water bottles are the easiest way to accomplish this. The size

of your water bottle will be determined by your cage and by how many rats you intend to supply. The standard 8-ounce bottle is sufficient for one rat. On wire cages, the bottles usually hang on the outside with an included piece of wire. However, on aquarium type cages, the bottle hangs on the inside.

A water bottle should be available so your rat has access to clean, fresh water at all times.

There are chewproof water bottles, and there are also holders that have chew guards. Most rats will chew the black cap area near the tube where the water comes out, so, usually, the water bottle holder will have a guard in that area only. Some rats are diligent, however, and may climb on the water bottle and chew the top as well. If they chew a minute hole in the top, the water bottle loses all of its suction, and the water will drip quickly out and soak your rat's home. A hot glue gun is a quick repair for small holes (but remember, rats like to eat glue, so be careful), and the black caps can sometimes be purchased at pet or feed supply stores. Water dishes are not recommended because they tip over easily and make a mess.

Food

Good nutrition is essential for a healthy rat and is discussed in detail in chapter 6. It is good to have some commercial rat or dry dog food on hand for your pet's arrival and to be aware of what people foods your rat can have.

Treats

Treats are fun to have on hand, but you should be aware of healthy snacks that your rat can have. As is the case for people, many of the foods rats like best aren't good for them.

Your rat will get hours of enjoyment from toys you purchase or make yourself.

Exercise Equipment

Wheels are a common form of exercise for rats and mice. Although mice are more likely to run on a wheel, there are some rats who enjoy this workout. Purchase or make a wheel that will be large enough for your rat. Many pet supply places carry rat wheels now. Some rats will use the wheel a lot when they're young and then less and less as they get older. If your rat is a fanatic wheel runner, don't be surprised by the appearance of a curly tail. It is common for a rat or mouse who runs on the wheel a lot to have a tail that naturally curls it, even when he is relaxed. If you have a squeaky wheel, especially if your ratty likes to serenade you with it at night, do not use a commercial lubricant or silicone spray. Use a vegetable-based oil to lubricate the metal-to-metal areas. Your ratty may snack on the oil, but it won't hurt him.

Do not put your rat in a commercial acrylic hamster ball. Besides the fact that rats are too big to fit in them, they are terrified of being in this unstable item and can overheat quickly due to panic and poor air circulation.

TOYS

Ratties love to play and you'll delight in their antics. Following are some good choices for cage toys:

- commercial bird toys

- small cat toys

- smooth wood pieces (for chewing)

- cardboard tubes (from toilet paper or paper towel rolls)

- large PVC pieces (from a home/plumbing supply store)

PET CARRIER

It is handy to have a specific carrier that you can put your rat in to keep him safe should you need to take him somewhere, such as to the vet. It can also be used for around the house when you are cage-cleaning or when the rat needs a break from small children and needs to be put up out of reach somewhere. There are many different kinds of carriers; what you choose should be based on what's available and on personal preference. Just like a cage, make sure that it is safe for the rat in that there are no sharp edges and something cannot "break into" it.

HUSBANDRY

Rats are extremely clean and enjoy staying that way. To help keep your pet's home clean and odor-free, it is recommended that you clean the entire cage at least once a week. This includes changing the bedding; washing and disinfecting the cage, water bottle and food dish (1 part bleach to 10 parts water is common); and replenishing bedding, nesting materials and so on. Cage cleaning can be necessary more often, depending on the size of your cage, your rat's personal housecleaning habits, how many ratties are in the cage and the type of bedding you use. If your rat gets upset by cage-cleaning, try to make it less stressful by leaving a bit of his old nesting material in with the new so that it smells like home.

On a daily basis, you should remove any fresh food that hasn't been eaten in a reasonable amount of time or it may spoil. You should also check your rat's dry food to see if it needs refilling. Be careful to discern whether the food has been eaten or your ratty just likes to stash it. You'll discover this when you clean the cage and a big pile of food shows up in what your rat thought was a great hiding place. You should also provide fresh water and clean out the corner of the cage that your rat uses to relieve himself. An easy way to do this is to take a plastic sandwich bag, turn it inside out and, with your hand on the outside of the baggy, grab the little handful in the corner. You can then turn the baggy right side out, which will enclose the handful of used bedding inside the bag. Then seal it and throw it away. After a few cleanings, it will seem like second nature, and your hand never touches the used bedding.

Feeding

Your Rat

Proper diet is essential to your rat's good health. Rats are omnivorous, which means that they will eat plant and animal material alike. As a general rule, Norway Rats prefer animal-based material. This is not to say that they don't also love plants, fruits, vegetables and grains. Unfortunately, for our little friends, they love food in general. Rats are one of the few animals that eat just for the sake of eating. They take their mealtimes seriously and enjoy each morsel. Like people, they also love junk food, like potato chips and candy. Junk food isn't any better for rats than it is for people, but, a rat will eat and eat. Who could forget Templeton the rat from *Charlotte's Web* and his eat-a-thon at the fairgrounds? He ate himself positively sick and loved every minute of it. Keeping your rat's love of food in mind will remind you to monitor her intake and make sure she eats a healthy diet with some table scraps and not the other way around.

Your Rat's Staple Diet

Your rat should be fed a staple diet that consists of a well-balanced vitamin and mineral supplemented kibble or block-type food. This kind of food gives rats the nutrients they need and is hard enough to

Lab blocks offer your rat complete nutrition and a way to keep teeth ground down.

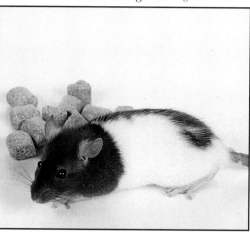

help keep their teeth ground down. Most rats like this type of food, and you will not usually have much trouble feeding it to them. Occasionally you will get a finicky eater, but a simple change of brand is usually all it takes. Remember, rats *love* food and aren't terribly picky as a general rule. The two main choices are lab blocks and dog kibble.

Lab blocks are a compressed form of a powder mix that includes the complete nutritional requirements for rodents. Lab blocks are usually available through pet stores, feed stores and, sometimes, your vet. This kind of food is the primary food laboratories use for their rats, and scientists clearly endorse it.

Dog kibble is simply commercially available dry dog food. The more expensive dry dog foods are not necessarily better for your rat. This is where you need to do some label reading. Rats should not have more than about 8% fat in their diet. Read the dog food labels and choose one that fits this requirement. Cat food should not be used unless you are feeding a pregnant or nursing mother with babies, as it is too rich in protein, fat and magnesium for a rat's diet.

Your rat should be able to feed freely on lab blocks or kibble and care should be taken to ensure that she has this type of food at all times, unless you have a rat that overeats. This is not usually the case with staple, healthy foods like these. Most overeating is done with treats, table food and grains.

Healthy Supplements

Rats love variety in their diets, and it will keep them healthy to give them foods that they would naturally

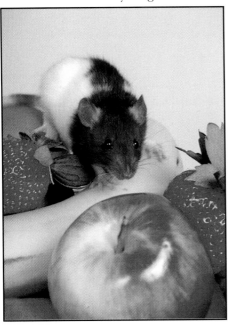

eat in the wild. In addition to their staple food, it is preferable that you add some variety to their diet to keep their nutritional values well rounded and the diet interesting. Try giving your rat a small amount of a different natural food each day. Some examples include the following:

Fruits Fruits are healthy, but are considered more of a treat. Some fruits, however, have higher vitamin levels than their vegetable counterparts. Be sparing with citrus fruits as they may make your rat's stom-

Supplement your rat's diet with nutritious fruits and vegetables.

ach acidic if given too often. Overfeeding of fruits can cause diarrhea, so be careful to give them in moderation. Always remember to wash fruit thoroughly before giving it to your ratty and to remove it promptly to avoid spoilage.

Vegetables Raw vegetables are good for your rat. They are full of natural vitamins and are a good source of liquid and roughage. Overfeeding green vegetables may cause diarrhea so give them in moderation. As with fruit, remember to wash vegetables thoroughly before giving them to your ratty and remove them promptly to avoid spoilage.

Grains Rats love whole grains such as bran, corn, uncooked oatmeal, rice and wheat. Breads and cereals (not the sugared kind) are good for them as well. Grains contain many vitamins and minerals in natural form that they would normally eat if in the wild.

Salt Rats do need salt, although they usually get all they need from their regular diet. If you are concerned about your rat getting enough salt and you live in a hot, dry area, it might be a good idea to purchase a commercial salt lick from the pet store. Some rats will use them.

Bones Rats can chew hard bones and enjoy them with gusto. Leftover cooked bones, such as those of beef or pork, can be great fun and a good source of nutrition for your rat. After your rat has methodically

An occasional bit of people food is a great treat for your rat.

sheared off all the meat, she can break into the bone and eat the marrow, which is rich in calcium. This practice is also good for her teeth. Try to avoid splintery bones such as chicken and fish. Cooked main chicken bones (such as the drumstick) are permissible if inspected and small splinters are removed first.

TABLE SCRAPS

Rats love people food. As a general rule, they can eat most anything, but there are a couple things to keep in mind. First of all, rats, like people, will overeat; your rat may not know when to stop and could become quite portly. Secondly, not all foods are good for them to eat in quantity. Moderation is always key. And, lastly, there are some special considerations of which to be aware.

Rats are unable to vomit, nor can they burp. So, what goes in must go all the way through. Some rat poisons

are successful due to this fact. By the time the rat real-
izes her mistake, she is unable to get rid of the poi-
soned food. While I'm sure you won't be feeding your
rat poison, it is important to consider that burping is a
common side effect of drinking soda pop. Rats love
soda and will make a beeline across the room to get
some. If your rat drinks enough soda, she could get discomfort and bloating from the gas in the carboniza-
tion. The best advice, of course, is not to let her have
any. Rats can be tricky, though, and get things that you
didn't intend for them to have. If you suspect your rat
may have drunk soda and is having discomfort, try to
help her stretch her stomach, walk a bit and move
around. This will help the gas move through her sys-

tem faster. It's also a good idea
to encourage her to drink some
water. This will not only stimu-
late her system to digest
quickly, but will help prevent
her from becoming dehy-
drated, which can occur with
soda as her only fluid.

You can use your rat as a sort of
rodent garbage disposal for
your fresh food scraps. They
love sheared corn cobs, apple
cores, pear cores, tomato ends,
squash ends and potato peel-
ings, to name a few. They will
eat most anything and are
delighted with trying new

*Your rat should
receive fresh food
and water daily.*

foods. After making a salad or similar item, let your rat
pick through the throwaways. They will be quite
impressed with all the good stuff you have. Of course,
as with any fresh food, always remember to wash it
thoroughly before giving it to your ratty and remove it
promptly after eating to avoid spoilage.

Because rats' metabolisms, eating habits and nutritional requirements are similar to humans', it is a
good rule of thumb to compare your rat's diet with
your own. If you wouldn't eat a cupcake every day for

breakfast, this is probably not terribly good for your rat, either. Rats can be prone to the same illnesses as people for overeating. These include heart disease, stroke, high cholesterol and obesity. Special occasions can warrant giving your rat the treats that she loves, but aren't good for her. This makes a treat more special for the two of you. Some of the more healthy people food that rats love include pasta, vegetables, low-fat cheese, yogurt, fruits, fish, breads, eggs and crackers. They will also eat scraps of meat and meat bones. Some bad foods they love, but should only have in moderation if at all include cookies, pastries, candy bars, regular cheese and most desserts. Use good judgment in feeding your rat and you will do fine. If it's good for you, it's probably good for her and if it isn't good for you, it probably isn't good for her.

TREATS

Treats are the way to your rat's heart. These can vary from table scraps, to rodent grain mixes, peanuts, sunflower seeds, dog biscuits or fish food. Treats should be rationed and doled out under specific circumstances. You can use these items for training, special occasions or simply for your quiet time. You should give your rat treats based on her weight and health. An overweight lazy rat isn't getting any benefit from a cupcake daily, and it is compounding her weight and activity status. If you need to cut down on your rat's treats, try choosing more healthy items. Often, your rat will like these just as much, we just forget to offer them. You can reserve her special favorite for once in awhile and, hopefully, she will become slimmer and healthier.

> ### DON'T LET YOUR RAT CHOKE
>
> Because rats have a poor gag reflex, choking is a serious problem. Avoid giving your rat sticky foods such as the following:
>
> - taffy
> - peanut butter
> - caramels
> - rolled fruit snacks
> - jelly beans
>
> If you see your rat choking, there is little you can do to help. Fortunately, rats usually manage to unstick the item.

If your rat is in a wire cage, it is not a good idea to feed her through the bars. Although it is tempting because it is so quick and easy, your rat will come to expect that whatever comes though the bars is a yummy for her. She will start grabbing without looking, and you may get nipped or even bitten if you smell like food. This practice is especially important if you have little ones around.

SUGARS

Rats don't really need extra sugars in their diet. Sugared foods such as most desserts, potato chips and candy-type items should be given very sparingly, if at all. In addition to the health factor regarding weight, tooth decay and lowered activity, rats are prone to addiction and can become dependent and quite rude if they don't get repeated helpings of their favorite junk food. Although dogs are allergic to an ingredient in chocolate, a rat doesn't seem to have the same problem. It was once thought that they must have the same allergy and that rats would probably react if they ate enough chocolate, but in recent years, there has been nothing to substantiate this idea. Nevertheless, a lot of chocolate, or sugars for that matter, isn't good for your ratty and care should be taken that she isn't able to access a large portion of them and overeat.

VITAMINS

Rats can be susceptible to vitamin deficiencies. This is not common, as they usually get all they need if they are fed a well-balanced diet. Rats, unlike humans, synthesize their own vitamin C, so you needn't specifically supplement it. They also will eat some of their droppings, like rabbits, to increase their absorption of nutrients, especially vitamin K, also naturally produced by your rat. But, if you have concerns or your rat is elderly and you are not sure if her body is still absorbing the nutrients in her diet as it should, you can buy a commercial vitamin supplement. This is usually a liquid that goes in the water bottle with an eyedropper and may be yellow or orange in color. Supplements will often stain the water bottle. Be sure to read the directions on the box. Some brands are only good for a certain time after they are mixed and then lose their potency.

Water

As discussed previously, water is crucial to a rat's well-being. They should have fresh water at their disposal at all times. Water bottles are preferred for this as they are the cleanest source. That is, spills are uncommon and water stays fresh inside. When you clean your cage, however, you will most likely need to clean your water bottle as well; use a bottle brush to do a thorough job. Don't forget the stopper and straw part. Your rat should be given fresh water daily, especially if you live in a warm or dry climate. If your rat is a chewer, there are several types commercially available that are "chew-proof," and there are also chew-guards to keep your rat from getting at your standard water bottle. Water in dishes is not recommended. It is easily spilled and can get shavings and waste kicked in it during housecleaning sessions.

chapter 7

Keeping Your
Rat
Healthy

Health care is very important for any pet and rats are no exception. Rats can be very sensitive and fragile under certain conditions, and they rely on their owners to keep them healthy and safe. It is important to be aware of what your rat's needs are and to know the signs of a healthy rat. If something is not right with your pet, you should be able to sense it immediately, even if you don't quite know what is different. A healthy rat will be bright-eyed, curious and inquisitive and have a sleek, glossy coat and good weight. Generally speaking, if your rat is given a clean home, a healthy diet, daily exercise, attention and an even temperature environment, he should be happy and in good health. However, even with the best of care, some illnesses or conditions can't be avoided and require human intervention with medications or treatments.

As a general rule, when something is wrong with your rat, unless you have specific experience and are confident in your abilities, take him to a vet. You don't want to gamble with your pet's life, and should it turn out badly, you will always wonder if you should have done something differently. Some conditions you may be able to diagnose yourself or describe to your vet; others may simply have vague symptoms and will require a vet with specific knowledge. Vets who specialize in small animals used to be few and far between, but this is changing and most areas today have at least one vet who is familiar with rats and their problems. Ask rat-owning friends for references, or call around to area vets and see if there is one who is comfortable treating rats. Should your rat need emergency attention, you will be glad you found a vet in advance.

Spending time with your rat and paying attention to his behavior will enable you to recognize quickly if something is wrong.

Some specific symptoms that signal a problem include the following: constant scratching, scabs on the body, bald patches, lumps, wounds, hunching over, not eating, listlessness, head tilted to one side, fur standing up, dull eyes, constant sneezing, red secretions around the eyes or nose, loss of weight or diarrhea. As you can see, some of the symptoms are easy to notice and some are not. This is one of the reasons why it is important to see your rat every day and take notice of his behavior and condition.

Let's discuss some of the more common health problems in rats. These descriptions of the health issues are not to encourage you to treat your pet yourself, but rather to enlighten you to the possibilities of what can happen and keep you informed to help your pet and your vet.

Common Health Concerns

GREASY, YELLOW, SCALY AREAS

Greasy patches are most common in males and are caused by an excessive secretion of the rat's oil glands. It is not damaging to the rat, although it isn't terribly attractive. A bath with mild shampoo usually takes care of the problem, although, if the rat's body is over-secreting, the problem will probably return.

Seek a veterinarian who has experience treating small animals.

PATCHY COLORS ON THE COAT

Patchiness of spots of lighter softer hair and darker coarser hair is usually just a sign of molting. Babies molt several times before adulthood and adults molt approximately every three months. It is more noticeable on the babies than the adults.

HAIR LOSS

Sometimes your rat may actually lose patches of hair. This can be caused by several different things. Some possible causes include the following:

- Your rat could have the rex line in its background. Sometimes when rexes molt, their hair will actually fall out in patches. Usually if this is the case, there will be peach fuzz at the area and the fur will grow back.

- The rat has hairless genes in his background. If this is the cause, after molting, the patch will usually be smooth and the hair may grow back sparsely or not at all.

- If a rat is getting patches on his body where the hair is being shortened unevenly, suspect that either a roommate or even the rat himself is chewing the fur. A roommate will usually do this on the sides or back of the rat. If the rat is doing this to himself, it is usually on the forelegs or chest area. In either scenario, this usually results from boredom. However, if one rat is chewing on another, it can be a sign of dominance.

- Hair loss can also be caused by excessive rubbing or itching. This can be from mites or lice, and you should refer to that section if you feel this is the case.

- It can simply be a behavioral trait where you have a rat that rubs a certain part of his body on the cage or on toys inside.

- Hair loss can also be caused by an allergy. If you suspect food allergies, refer to the food allergy section. If you don't feel this is the case, suspect bedding, household cleaners, lotions and soaps (on your hands and transferred to you pet) and anything else you can think of that could be topical.

BE READY FOR THE VET

Should you need to take your rat to the vet, help your rat and your vet out by noting some general facts. For example, you should be able to tell your vet the following:

- how old your rat is
- what symptoms you've noticed
- your rat's typical behavior
- how your rat is being affected by his current condition
- when you first noticed the problem
- how long you think your rat has had the problem
- what steps you have taken to treat it
- what illness or condition you think it is and why
- what you've been feeding your rat
- where your rat is being housed (inside or outside; wire cage or aquarium)

Treatment for any of these causes isn't always necessary unless there are special circumstances and the results are serious.

RED STAINS ON THE COAT

Red staining can be caused by your rat's bedding—for example, if you are using cedar (not a good idea, please see the Bedding section in chapter 5)—and this staining will wash off. Another cause is the rat's saliva from cleaning himself. There is an ingredient in rats' saliva that is a reddish color and can be transferred onto their coat during their usual grooming routines. It is most likely on areas where they lick directly—the sides of the back and rump area and legs—but can be transferred anywhere. It is most noticeable on white rats. Some rats are more prone to this than others. Presumably there are different levels of the secretion for each individual rat. Some rats that help groom others as well as themselves may spread the wealth around, and you may get red staining spots on everyone in the cage. Be gentle with them, they think they're helping.

SCABS

If you spot scabs on your ratty, it definitely indicates that something is amiss. Most people assume that the sight of scabs means that the rat has mites, but this is not always the case. We'll discuss mites first, however, because they are the most well-known cause.

Mites

Mites are small parasitic creatures that usually come from wood sources. They can be present in shavings, even if the bedding is packaged commercially. For this reason, it is never a good idea to make a rat's home from wood. Mites are difficult to see with the naked eye, but it is possible. They appear as red dots moving on your rat's skin. Occasionally, with a severe infestation, you can see them on the wood. Mites are the most common parasite for the Norway Rat. Scabs from mites will usually be in places the rat can reach with his hind legs, such as the back and shoulders. If the majority of the scabs are in those locations, chances are that mites are to blame.

Home treatment will include the cleaning and sanitizing of your rat's home. This means you must take your rat's cage apart and scrub it thoroughly. Disinfect it with something safe like a solution of diluted bleach (1 part bleach to 10 parts water is the typical recommendation) and rinse it thoroughly with hot water. After rinsing your cage, if you're lucky enough to be in a warm climate, let it dry in the sun. There are commercial disinfectants made specifically for animals, but be careful not to use any household cleaners. They can be toxic to your rat, even when dry, and some have side effects such as hair loss.

Mites from wood sources can infect your rat, causing him a great deal of discomfort.

You will also need to clean and disinfect your rat's food dishes, water bottle and any toys in his cage. Any paper, cardboard or wooden items should be tossed. If your rat has certain places in your home where he often runs or hides out, it is a good idea to treat them with a commercial flea treatment.

The rat himself must be bathed and dipped. You can bathe your rat using any mild commercial shampoo. For dipping, you should use a commercial dip that states it is safe for use on kittens. Keep in mind that rats clean themselves just like cats do. Whenever you must get something similar, always choose a label that's safe for cats. Mix a small portion of the dip and after bathing and drying your rat, use a cotton ball to soak your rat's body. Starting at the head, behind the ears,

make a ring around the neck and work your way back.
Make sure to soak your rat's entire body. Don't rinse
him off; instead, let your rat dry naturally while trying to keep him from licking himself. Blow dryers
are acceptable to use if you use the low-heat, low-air
setting and don't put it too close or aim it at your
rat's face. All of this intervention, bathing, dipping,
sanitizing of cage, etc. must be done on the same day.
Like dogs and cats with fleas, you have to break the
cycle entirely.

Be forewarned that these steps may not always take
care of the problem. You may need to take your rat to
the vet for treatment. Commonly, the vet will take a
skin scraping from your rat and have it analyzed by a
lab to confirm that it has mites. If it is positive, your vet
will usually treat your rat with Ivermectin, and you will
probably have to repeat the sanitizing and cleaning of
your rat's cage.

Lice

Lice are not as common as mites, but can infest your
rat. Rats are usually infected by being in close quarters
with birds, such as chickens. This can be the case even
if the birds have been moved. Lice are not easy to see
either, but usually appear as small, gray moving insects.
The main symptom separating mites from lice is the
presence of eggs. Lice will lay their eggs along the hair
shaft of the animal. These eggs can easily be seen and
are often mistaken for dust. If the eggs are so small that
you cannot easily distinguish the shape of a teardrop
from an irregular dust particle, blow gently on the
affected area. If it is dust, the white spots move in the
wind. If they are lice eggs, they will not budge as lice
use a type of glue or cementing technique to keep
their eggs attached.

Treatment for lice is the same as for mites. Be aware
that while the treatment will kill adult lice and the
loose eggs, often the eggs will remain cemented to the
hair shaft. They may stay there until the rat molts. It is
possible to comb them out with a fine-toothed lice
comb, but for our rat friends, this is uncomfortable

and sometimes painful. As always, if there is any question or problem, consult your vet.

Food Allergies

Food allergies are another common reason for scabs. Most often the scabs are on areas of the body where the rat won't scratch incessantly, but will often rub. Common places are under the chin or on the sides of the body. Most food allergies are caused by an excess of protein or pure fats in the diet. This makes the rat itchy and results in "hot spots" that he scratches or rubs to bring relief. Treatment is, essentially, adjusting your rat's diet.

First, evaluate what you feed your rat. If there are other family members, consult them as well; some family members may be giving your rat treats unbeknownst to you. Check the protein content of your commercialized food, such as dog food or prepared rat food. Try to keep the protein content at about 8% or less. Observe the amount of sunflower seeds and peanuts (a big contributor) included in the diet. Take into account any junk food you've been giving him, such as potato chips.

The next step is to take your rat off his usual diet and give him a very bland diet of rice, pasta and vegetables for a few days. Make sure he has plenty of clean, fresh water to help clean out his system. Incorporate the healthy parts of his diet slowly over the next few days and see if his skin begins to clear up. You can use a topical ointment for his sores. Discuss with your family the importance of diet and what your rat can and cannot have so that everyone understands. Most rats with these types of food allergies will always be sensitive to diet changes. Make sure everyone knows what treats they can offer.

EYE INFECTIONS

It is not common for rats to have problems with eye injuries or infections, but they do happen. The usual culprits are dust, a cold or an injury caused by a scratch or even a "sharp" part of a shaving. Treatment at home involves cleaning the eye with a clean, warm washcloth and using a vet-recommended antibiotic eye ointment. If your rat has some grayish white areas in the eye, these are probably cataracts, and there is no treatment for them. These often appear in elderly rats, but can also occur in younger rats as they are hereditary. If your rat's eye is protruding, do not try to treat him at home; take him to the vet immediately. There is obviously something more serious going on that can't be seen.

If your rat has pink eyes, like an albino, or one of the light colors, they can become swollen due to excessive sunlight. If you've had your rat outside in the sun and this happens, move him to the shade immediately. Keep him cool and quiet and just watch him carefully. His eyes will usually return to normal in a couple hours. Make sure you keep him in the shade when outside for any length of time.

VAGINAL BLEEDING

Vaginal bleeding doesn't occur often, but is not uncommon, either. This is not a normal condition. Female rats do not have periods or seasons when they bleed. If you see blood in this area and your rat is pregnant, it could be the start of her labor, a miscarriage or labor distress. If your rat is not pregnant, the most common causes are tumors. Uterine tumors, unfortunately, are common in female rats. You will need to consult your vet to determine how advanced the tumors are and if there is any treatment. Surgery is possible, but is often expensive and usually does not keep tumors from reoccurring.

WOUNDS

Wounds can be caused by many things; the most common cause is a rat fight between males. If you have two males together and they have fought diligently enough to cause a bloody wound, they should be separated immediately. Significant bites mean business and there is usually no "making up"; these two just aren't going to get along. If the wound is deep, you will probably see the initial skin opening and then another layer of tissue that is off-white to gray. This is the muscle layer, and if you are able to see it, you need to take your rat to the vet for stitches. Wounds this deep are much more prone to infection. If it is a relatively mild wound, you should clean it and try to keep the rat as quiet as possible. To clean the area, use a soft cloth and wipe gently with warm water. After you feel that any excess blood and/or shavings have been removed, mix equal parts of hydrogen peroxide with water and rinse this solution over the area. The peroxide will bubble and fizz as it kills the bacteria. You may need to do this more than once, perhaps twice a day for three days. Basically, a good initial washing is enough, and the wound should scab over and heal itself.

ABSCESSES

An abscess starts out as a wound. It can be a wound that you saw and took care of or a small wound that you didn't notice. For example, sometimes a rat will get an injury that cuts into the skin without leaving a large opening. This area gets bacteria inside and the wound becomes infected or "abscesses." The area will swell and have a squishy feel with a hard knot in the middle. There is usually a scab on the top of the abscess. When bacteria gets inside a wound, instead of healing normally, the wound scabs over and starts to swell.

This can occur in a relatively small amount of time and can seem to pop up overnight. Unfortunately, this abscess must be drained regularly to get it to heal. Unless you've done this before, take your rat to the vet and have him or her demonstrate the procedure. Basically, it involves scraping off the scab, squeezing the abscess to drain it of the infected pus, washing the area and disinfecting it. This is not for the faint of heart. Besides the obvious distastefulness, it is painful to your rat and is difficult to do. It must be pointed out that it has to be done, however, or the rat is in danger of having the infection spread to his whole system.

RINGTAIL

Ringtail is a disease that is usually related to low humidity in the air, which causes the tail to dehydrate. The tail may look constricted as if someone put several rubber bands around it. The scales can slough off, and the tip can become damaged and fall off. Take your rat to the vet for care. The vet will help you determine arrangements in your rat's cage to increase the moisture, but the damage to his tail will remain permanent.

EAR INFECTIONS

Ear infections are often a side effect of a cold or respiratory infection. A rat holding his head cocked to one side is a common symptom. Ear infections should be treated with antibiotics immediately, so seek the counsel of your vet. If untreated, the ear infection can destroy the inner ear, which governs the rat's equilibrium. This condition is commonly referred to as Wry Neck. The rat should still be treated for the infection so he is in good health, but there is no remedial treatment for the destroyed eardrum. Rats with this condition can still live normal, healthy lives. In some cases, however, the destruction is so great that the rat will often fall over and sometimes roll to one side uncontrollably many times before being able to get up. If your rat has a severe case, please consult your vet for advice on the extent of his comfort.

There is a behavior in pink-eyed rats where they will sway slightly while standing still. This is thought to be due to their poor eyesight and the concentration it takes for their eyes to focus.

DIARRHEA

Rats' normal stools should be firm, solid and dry. If they become loose, soft or runny, there could be a diarrhea problem. Ordinarily, diarrhea is caused by too many greens. If you cut the greens from your rat's diet, the problem should clear up in a day or two. If this is the case, then you should adjust future diet items accordingly. If it doesn't clear up, consult your vet. There are some internal infections that can cause this. Occasionally, when rats are in unfamiliar surroundings, they may get rather odorous diarrhea from nervousness. The most common situation is when transporting them to a show. Once your rat returns home or to his familiar area, his stools usually revert to normal.

DEHYDRATION

Dehydration is not common for healthy rats. If it happens, it is usually due to a lack of available water or occurs in a sick animal that is refusing fluids. The rat will appear thin, listless and hunched and will usually refuse water. To give your rat water, it is suggested that you mix a little sugar in and use an eyedropper. Put the dropper in the rat's mouth facing the side or the cheek. Don't put it straight facing the throat or you could choke your rat. Gently squeeze approximately two drops at a time and encourage the rat to lick the dropper. Sometimes it takes a little while before they respond. If you are getting no response and your rat doesn't look good, call your vet right away.

Diarrhea can be caused by too many greens. It will correct itself once the rat's diet returns to normal.

HEATSTROKE

Heatstroke is very dangerous to rats. They do best in even mid-temperatures, 60° to 80°F, and can easily overheat in temperatures over 90°F. In the first stages of heatstroke, the rat will lie flat out on his stomach, panting with eyes wide open. He will often drool, and the chin and neck area may become very wet. If a rat is

93

in an aquarium, he will often stand or lie against the glass with his underside (his very wet underside) touching the glass. He will usually not drink even if water is available because often the water is warm. If the rat is not cooled during this time, he will eventually overheat and lapse into a coma. Death is not far away at this point. If he is so hot that he becomes comatose, it is hard to bring him back; he'll probably die of heart failure.

Should you spot your rat in one of these states, get him out immediately and start cooling him. Take him to a cool spot and start sponging him down with cool, not cold, water. You want to lower the rat's temperature as fast as possible without throwing him into shock. When the rat perks up a little, have him drink some water on his own or with the eyedropper. Make sure he has cool water in his cage, and keep him quiet and cool for the rest of the day.

Figure out why the rat overheated and make some changes for your cage requirements or location. In warm areas, rat owners are encouraged to freeze plastic bottles three-quarters full of water and place one in the cage each morning. The rat will lay near, on or even over them to help keep him cool.

Rats, like all rodents, have teeth that grow continually. Provide food and chewtoys that will help your rat keep his teeth worn down.

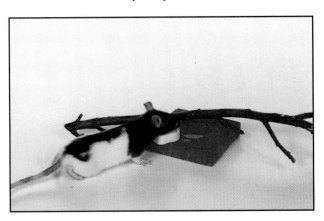

OVERGROWN TEETH

Rats do not usually get overgrown teeth, but it does happen. Rats' teeth grow throughout their lives, which is why rats constantly chew and gnaw. Ordinarily, your rat's diet and playthings (and things he's not supposed to play with) will keep his teeth healthy and at a reasonable length. If, however, you suspect that your rat's teeth have overgrown, see your vet immediately. Symptoms include weight loss, untouched treats and possibly swollen jaws. Sometimes, teeth will need to be clipped and this is best done by a vet. Rats can also have deformities in their jaws that can cause eating problems. This isn't always initially apparent and sometimes shows up later in the rat's life.

RESPIRATORY INFECTIONS

Respiratory infections are the most frightening to seasoned rat owners because by the time you see any symptoms, it's often too late. Rats are very prone to respiratory infections. These can range from the standard cold to the dreaded Mycoplasma Pneumonia. Most rats will sneeze and the occasional sneeze is nothing for concern. If the sneezing has gone so far as to be constant, producing mucous or if your rat looks blurry-eyed, you should pay a visit to the vet. Most respiratory infections can be treated with antibiotics. You will need to consult with your vet to determine what illness is suspected and the correct antibiotic treatment. Often, if the infection has spread, the rat will make a "snuffling" or "rattling" sound in his chest when he breathes. While this is cause for concern and should be checked, sometimes this can be from past illnesses that have created scar tissue. The scar tissue can interfere with the lungs' normal breathing patterns. A very sick rat with Mycoplasma or other pneumonia will exhibit several signs stated at the beginning of this chapter: hair standing up, eyes dull, listlessness, loss of weight, constant sneezing. Your little rat needs help.

Keep in mind that respiratory illnesses are *highly* infectious and care should be taken with any other rats you have. The sick one (and any cagemates) should be quarantined. Be on the lookout for these symptoms when acquiring a new rat, or you could infect your whole group. Any rat that is suspected to have a respiratory infection should be treated immediately and given the full dose of antibiotics. You also need to simultaneously dose everyone in the cage. If you don't complete the whole dosing treatment, you risk weakening the virus, but not killing it, which will make it more difficult to combat the next time.

As for that red stuff around the eyes—although it looks suspiciously like blood, it isn't. The gland behind the eye that keeps it lubricated manufactures a substance called poripherin. This lubricant is emitted to keep the eyes and lids moist and is red in color. When the rat's eyes are watery from sneezing, the gland increases its production and you begin to see the red color.

A red nose could be from the rat pawing at his nose from the constant sneezing, the red poripherin again or it could be the aftermath of little broken blood vessels during sneezing fits.

TUMORS

Unfortunately, rats are prone to tumors. One of the reasons they are used in research is their affinity for cancerous growths. Most growths that rats get are benign and don't give them much bother. They will live their life normally, ignoring the gigantic lump attached to an odd place. If a tumor gets too big and bothersome, they may start chewing on it. This behavior should prompt you to take some action, as the rat's quality of life is being compromised. Tumors can be surgically removed and the rats recover from surgery quite well. Before surgical intervention, however, you need to take into account the age of the rat and the size and type of the tumor. Benign tumors are usually attached to fatty areas and generally don't affect the rat's organs or other physical functions. Removing a benign tumor is usually no trouble for the surgeon or the rat. Malignant tumors, however, are usually internal and attached to one or more organs. Removing a malignant tumor is difficult and most often doesn't buy much time. The cancerous cells will simply grow quickly somewhere else. Tumors tend to be hereditary, but many breeders have specifically bred out animals that have grown tumors. However, if your rat lives long enough, he will probably get tumors simply due to age.

INJURIES

Your rat may get injured at some time. Rats are fragile and small and must be handled with care, but accidents do happen. As with most maladies, prevention is the best cure for this. Use your common sense and don't let small children play unsupervised with your rat. Never pick a rat up by his tail—the tail can break off or the sheath skin covering can come off. Avoid contact with larger prey animals (cats and dogs) without close supervision. And try to be aware of any potential hazards (areas where he could fall, poisonous plants, electrical cords, etc.). Above all, if your rat is harmed, get him medical attention right away. Whether the problem simply needs some washing and first aid attention or requires a trip to the vet, take care of it immediately to avoid other problems down the road.

SPAYING AND NEUTERING

It is possible to spay or neuter your rat. Of course there are pros and cons to each option. There is currently no evidence to support the possibility that spaying or neutering will lengthen a rat's life. The main benefits are simply to be rid of the sex organs, which could become cancerous or develop other problems. The main drawback is that they must be put under general anesthesia, which is always a risk.

For female rats, the procedure is quite invasive, but can keep them from getting uterine, mammary or ovarian cancer. Keep in mind that this is abdominal surgery, after all, and can be traumatic. For males, the usual reasons for neutering are to allow him to live with a female and not breed. Although, the procedure for the male is not as invasive, it is still more complicated than for other animals and must be done under general anesthetic. In addition to the other concerns, it may be difficult to locate a vet who will be comfortable doing the procedure and it could be costly.

The Elderly Rat

An aged rat will have special concerns just like people. You may need to adjust his diet to keep his weight up and keep an eye on his teeth to see that he is wearing them down properly. Your older rat will be more sensitive to heat and cold, so care should be taken to ensure that he is comfortable during all types of weather. Older rats will often shy away from being held by children as their bones and bodies begin to feel fragile. Most importantly, keep your rat happy and comfortable in his final time. Make sure you observe him regularly and note if you feel he isn't

Your older rat may not be up to the tricks he was as a youngster, but he is still a devoted pet.

doing well or if he is experiencing any pain. Often, by the time a rat allows you to see his discomfort or pain, it is too late to alleviate it. If you must take a final trip to the vet, discuss it with your family *first* and allow each family member to come to terms with it and make their own peace.

A WORD ABOUT EUTHANASIA

Nobody likes to think about having their beloved pet put to sleep, but it is important to consider the quality of the animal's life. Your rat is trusting you to give him the best possible care, and that can sometimes mean that putting him to sleep is best. This is not a decision to be made lightly. Please seek the advice of your vet, family members and friends. Carefully weigh the facts and be honest with yourself. Follow your heart because it knows. When your rat is having more difficulties than fun and frolic, or more pain than peace, you need to consider your alternatives. Keep in mind that this is a personal decision and no one can give you certain criteria to follow. Follow your instincts and use your best judgment.

Enjoying

Your

part three

Rat

chapter 8

Understanding
Your
Rat

Rats are highly social creatures that seek out companionship, enjoy human company and are loyal, affectionate friends. By understanding some of their behaviors, you can develop a strong personal bond with your ratty. Many people are surprised by the intensity of affection they feel for their rat and the amount of love they receive back. Keeping your rat healthy and happy will result in a mutually rewarding relationship for both of you.

Rat Behavior

In order to understand some of your rat's behaviors, we must remember where the rat came from and what her instincts are. Rats have survived for thousands of years on their wits and resources. It is their intelligence, adaptability and quick thinking that have enabled them to survive catastrophes, such as plagues, famines and exterminations, that would have wiped out other animals.

RATS IN THE WILD

In the wild, it is common for the rat to live in a colony or "rat pack." Due to their sociability, rats enjoy communal living and seek out other rats. They function as part of the group, often taking turns and helping other rats who are ill or injured. The female rats help mothers in the group care for their young and males will help baby-sit.

Rats often live in complex housing arrangements in the wild. That is, they will seek out a cool, dark location and set about redecorating it. This can be anything from a series of tunnels in the ground to an empty storage room in a building. Basements are a favorite location for the rats, because they're inside; also, basements are not heavily populated by people and stay cool. Rats will usually seek an area large enough to have a communal place where all the rats in the colony can come and socialize, but also have space where they can be by themselves. If you ever look at a cage of domestic rats, you'll notice that sometimes there's a giant pile of rats in the corner, and then other times there are rats strewn everywhere.

Rat behavior, like their climbing ability, is derived from skills they used to survive in the wild.

The rat's ability to avoid predators is based largely on her intelligence and natural reluctance to take

103

chances on new things. When a rat is confronted by a new situation, you can often observe her looking, taking in the details and deciding whether it's worth investigating further. These are crucial decisions when the new item is, for example, a rat trap. While a rat's eyesight is not great, her sense of smell and her hearing work very well. You'll often see rats with their noses held high gathering in smells, or frozen like rabbits listening intently. This is their primary source of getting information about their surroundings. Rats' quick thinking and agile bodies have gotten them out of many scrapes. Holding a frightened rat who is trying desperately to get away can resemble trying to hang on to a wet bar of soap. They keep running, pulling and pushing until they get loose and can run to safety. Their climbing and jumping skills serve them well in finding safe places to hide when avoiding capture by man or other animals.

Rats' curiosity can often be their downfall.

A rat's main instinct when frightened is to get away. Although it happens, they rarely bite, even under extreme circumstances. Their curiosity can be their downfall, however, for you will often see a scaredy-cat peeking out from her hiding place to survey the situation. Rats can't help their inquisitiveness and want to see and know everything they can.

SOCIAL ORDER

Within each rat colony, whether it consists of two or 200 rats, there is a pecking order. Dominance is established between the males of the pack as well as between the females. While most females yield control to any male, there are exceptions where you will have a "nerd" that seems to have some type of personality

defect. Nobody likes him and he is pushed around by most of the colony. These outcasts tend to be pitiful whiners, crying in a series of resigned squeals, and they cower when most any rat approaches. The solution to this, I've found, is to place the rat in a new colony with considerably younger rats. This way there is no question of hierarchy as the older rat gets to be the boss by default, and they all seem to get along fine.

When determining pecking order in males, rats will usually stand on their hind legs with their noses raised in the air, perhaps in an

ESCAPE

Rats are good escape artists and sometimes escape from their cages. As rats are nocturnal, this usually happens at night. It is very common for your rat to crawl in bed with you. If your rat escapes, leave her cage door open so that she can return (it is her home, after all). If you are sitting watching TV or reading, your rat will most likely seek you out and you'll see her peeking out watching you. Talk to her softly and gently approach her. Unless she is still a little nervous or scared, she should come right out to you, and then you can give her the naughty rat lecture.

attempt to be the tallest. There will sometimes be pushing in the face with the front legs and some squeaking as each rat stands and surveys the situation. There can also be karate kicks from the hind legs as they will raise them to ward off any attacks. Often, one rat will lower himself and back down and the show is over. If this doesn't happen and an actual fight breaks out, the aggressor usually drops and lunges for the underside of his opponent biting him on the stomach area. These are nasty bites that usually tear through the muscle tissue as well as break the skin. Once there is a bite, the brawl begins and can last from a second to several minutes. There is much rolling around, squeaking, biting and flying bedding. If other rats are in the area, they will stay out of the way and watch worriedly. If one rat decides to yield to the other (this is usually the rat on the bottom of the rolling bundle when it stops), the two fighting will stop rolling and freeze in whatever spot they've landed for a staring contest. This cements the fact that the one rat gave in and is lower than the "winning" rat. When the dominant rat feels his point has been made, he will slowly climb off and the rat on the bottom will get up and retreat to a corner to lick his wounds. Often the other rats will go to the individual and help him clean. Sometimes he will let them, other times there is a short squabble of "leave me alone" language. These fights can go down the line to the bottom until the entire colony has a place.

The females will establish their own hierarchy amongst themselves. It is uncommon for their ritual to end in blood fighting, but it does happen. Usually, the females will start in the stand-up mode similar to the males and one will yield dominance to the other. If the females do get into brawls, it is not usually to the extent of the males. Bite wounds, if any, are usually superficial. Most often, their disagreements are merely yelling fights that result in a lot of squeaking.

Spend time with your rat and try to understand what she is trying to communicate to you.

Understanding What Your Rat Is Telling You

Your rat will go to great efforts to communicate with you. You are her head rat, and your opinion is very important. Often, it is not easy to figure out what your rat is trying to say, but she definitely has something in mind that she's trying to tell you. Here is a key that may help.

Teeth Grinding Sometimes your rat will make this sound when she is relaxing with you. It is interpreted as a sign of contentment. Her head will vibrate slightly and she will grind her teeth noticeably at irregular intervals. Often, the eyelids will lower a bit, as if relaxing. It is speculated that this may also be an inherent behavior for keeping the teeth worn down. In any case, since the rat only does it when relaxed, you should be flattered if your ratty feels comfortable enough to sit with you and grind her teeth.

Teeth Chattering This is a loud clicking sound. Rats usually reserve this sound for when they are angry at another rat. They may exhibit other behaviors in addition to the clicking and may also hiss.

Tail Swishing Some rats will swing their tail around when they are excited and running at playtime. It's almost an exaggeration of counter-balancing. They will often do this when they are on your shoulder and you will get a tail in the face when this happens. Your rat thinks she's playing with you.

Tail Slapping If your rat is frozen still and her tail is shivering, shaking, convulsing or slapping the floor in short movements, she is very angry, threatened or annoyed. This agitation is usually caused by an invasion of territory—another rat on her turf. However, she may exhibit this behavior toward a dog or cat as well. Remove the offending party or give the rat something to crawl into until she calms down.

SQUEAKING

Rats communicate by a series of squeaks that are often too high pitched for humans to hear. Rats can often identify each other by squeaking greetings as well as by smell and touch. Some rats are naturally more squeaky than others; this is simply a personality trait. There are different types

---

THE MEANING OF SQUEAKING

Of the squeaks that we can hear, the most common squeaks and the reasons for them follow:

The Quick Squeak: This is usually an expression of surprise or hurt, like when you stub your toe and say "ouch." It is simply a short little squeak and is usually not a serious one. If you hear it, you should check your rat for injury just in case.

The Long High-Pitched Squeak: This is usually used when a rat is frightened out of her wits or is being injured and is unable to get away, like when she gets her tail caught. This squeak usually signifies injury or extreme trauma. It is often used when fighting. If you hear this squeak, check your rat right away as she may need first aid.

The Whiny Medium-Pitched Squeak: This is usually used when the rat is unhappy about what is going on, but isn't really being injured. This squeak usually occurs when you are trying to give her medicine she doesn't like, when she is being dominated by another rat or when she has a cherished piece of food and is being chased by her roommate. Some rats use this more often than others.

of squeaks, but, of course, we can only respond to the ones that we can hear. Because of their ability to hear high-pitched squeaks, electric devices that emit such high-frequency sounds often force rats to leave an area. Rats may become annoyed with these sounds and have been observed in lab situations trying to get as far away from these high-pitched noises as they can.

Cleanliness

Your rat is a very clean animal. She will regularly clean her house and bed as well as her coat and body. She licks hers forepaws with her saliva and uses it to clean her fur and scrub her face. She washes behind her ears and carefully smooths everything back in place.

Rats are meticulous groomers.

Rats can get so obsessive that they may clean a roommate who doesn't want to be cleaned. The aggressive one will hold the other down and hurriedly chew and lick to clean the fur. The rat being cleaned usually squeaks, but this doesn't daunt the cleaner. It's as if she thinks it's for her roommate's own good. Sometimes, if you have an unfamiliar smell on you, your rat may clean herself after you handle her. This is not to offend, for often your rat will decide to clean you, too. She may lick you and fuss with your hair to help it lay right. She thinks she is doing you a great favor.

Chewing

Chewing is an important part of a rat's behavior. As you know, rats' teeth grow continuously throughout their lives and must be kept worn down. Because of this, it is a rat's natural desire to chew a lot. How much your rat chews seems to be built into her personality. Some will chew anything in sight, including wood, plastic, clothing, cardboard and anything else they can get their teeth into. Others are content to chew on things in their cage and rarely lay a tooth on anything else. Unfortunately, your rat does not discern what is a good thing to chew on and what is a bad thing. Therefore, this can be dangerous to your rat if she runs loose in your home. She can chew electrical cords and holes through screens to the outdoors. She can also wreak havoc with your furniture. It may be cute that your rat hides behind your throw pillows on your couch until you turn one over and there's a nice ratty hole there. Sometimes there's even a nice stash of food or loose items. Since your rat is driven by instinct to do this, training or punishment isn't an option. You simply have to take precautions to prevent her from doing it.

Marking

Some rats will mark their territory with little urine drops. This is most often done by males, but is also done by some females. The rat simply leaves tiny little urine drops as she lumbers along. This is mostly an inconvenience as it doesn't really have much odor, cause much dampness or stain. It can require regular clean-up, like wiping smooth surfaces or laundering. If your rat is prone to this behavior, it is probably easiest to throw a towel or similar item over the area where your rat will be playing. This will help save your furniture. If your rat runs on the carpeting, you may need to have your carpet cleaned a bit more frequently and use a baking soda–based deodorizing powder when vacuuming.

Your rat needs out-of-cage play-time with you every day.

Outside Playtime

You need to set up a playtime for your rat each day. Your rat should get a least an hour of "out" time with you and more time if she is an only rat. She will enjoy socializing with you, interacting with you and even playing with you. Rats are very playful and enjoy games like wrestling and chase. Rats are just about always ready to come out, and will adjust to your schedule because they cherish their time with you. If you have varied hours and need to take your rat out at different times, she won't mind. If you have a regular schedule and she will come out the same time every day, she will be poised and ready for you.

chapter 9

Training Tips and Tricks

Due to the great intelligence and agility of rats, training them to do tricks is not difficult and can actually be great fun. It is very rewarding when your rat knows what you are trying to tell him and responds. When he does these things for you, you definitely know he is your rat buddy.

Natural Talents

There are several reasons why rats are such good acrobats and do so well with training. Before we discuss training, let's review your rat's natural talents.

ATHLETIC ABILITY

Rats are deftly athletic. They are wonderful climbers and excellent jumpers. If your rat is out to play in your home, you'll be amazed at how swiftly he leaps from the coffee table to the couch, climbs quickly to the top, hops from cushion to cushion, skids down to the end table and snaps up your snack. Upon retrieving such a prize, he'll take the same route back, holding his head high with the treasure. If the prize is large, your rat may hop, almost like a kangaroo, to a safe place where he can stash the loot.

Rats' strong, broad feet contribute to their athleticism.

There are several physical characteristics of the rat that make him such an excellent athlete.

Hind legs   A rat's hind legs are bent at an angle like most rodents. Because of this, rats have great jumping power and spring action similar to those of a frog.

Feet   A rat's hind feet are broad and long. This gives him a good base for landing after jumps. He also has good balance when standing. His front feet are shaped like hands and are extremely adept at grabbing and holding. They can find hand-holds in very small areas.

Claws   Claws are good for gripping items and for climbing.

Senses   A rat's hearing and smell are very keen, which helps him to identify a dangerous situation. Eyesight is poor, and is most effective in the evening light. Rats have a heightened sense of touch and can often feel the slightest ruffle of their hair. Taste is, of course, the most concentrated sense. Rats love food.

Whiskers   A rat's whiskers are a good sensor. They can detect which way the wind is blowing and changes in temperature. It is said that a rat's whiskers are as long as his body is wide. If his whiskers will fit into a hole, his body can too. Of course this theory doesn't always work as obese rats' whiskers don't continue to grow, nor do they get smaller if they lose weight. However, the general theory is plausible; this could account for rats being able to get into small places without getting stuck. They just ask their whisker-meter if they'll fit.

Tail When it comes to athletic ability, the tail is, perhaps, a rat's most important physical attribute. He uses it primarily for balance. It is easy to observe the rat balancing and counter-balancing when he is teetering on a small area. The tail is also used to respire heat to help avoid heatstroke, and as a gripper in climbing. If you feel a rat's tail (not a lot of people's favorite part of the rat anatomy), you'll notice that it is covered with scales and soft hair. If you

A rat's tail is a tool for touch and balance.

run your fingers down the tail from base to tip, you'll find it's quite smooth. However, if you run your fingers from tip to base, you'll discover that the scales pop up and feel almost rough and prickly. When a rat is climbing, you'll notice their tail moving swiftly in all directions to counter-balance. What you may not initially notice is that it also is rubbing against the item that's being climbed on as a sort of stabilizer. It helps the rat get a good grip.

INTELLIGENCE

In addition to their athletic abilities, rats are considered highly intelligent. A rat has the unique ability to learn from his own and other rats' experiences. Rats have good memories and will often draw on their past to determine their current actions. For example, if a rat saw another go into a live animal trap and get caught, he may remember that the rat was unable to get out of the caged area. Consequently, if a rat came upon an item that looked similar to the trap, he would probably not go anywhere near it, connecting it to the previous experience.

Some consider rats to be more intelligent than dogs. They have excellent problem-solving skills, will often take the time to weigh options and invariably will pick the shortest route to accomplish their goal. Since the rat looks for the quickest, easiest way to do something, you have to make training worth his while. Treats or attention are great rewards.

Rats are extremely intelligent creatures who learn from their experiences.

Training Possibilities

Rats can be easily trained to do tricks for you. They love to please and are especially interested if there's food involved. Rats are quite smart and once they understand what you want them to do, they are usually quite cooperative. Everyone has heard of rats running incredible mazes, but did you know that rats can do other tricks as well? Some colleges will assign projects involving teaching rats. The student must obtain and raise a rat and teach him a complicated series of tricks to complete a certain script. These students spend countless hours with their subject reinforcing the training as well as the behaviors. They also create the sets for their rat's interaction. Their final exam is a presentation of their rat's accomplishments. These classes have gained such popularity that the final exam is often profiled on the news and the class sometimes has a waiting list. Tricks include riding in a boat, raising a flag, jumping in a certain order, riding on motorized mini-cars and responding to verbal commands. These tricks are all done one after the other without reinforcement in between each task. Although some of the students' tricks are quite complicated, there are lots of basic ones you can teach your pet at home.

GAMES

Rats love to play games and will do so with other rats as well as with you. Females are more playful than males, but both enjoy interaction with people. A game is usually something that is based on a rat's behavior and brings enjoyment to both you and your rat. When playing with your rat, don't be surprised to find yourself rolling on the floor with laughter. Your little rat can be quite comical when he gets worked up. Rats tend to get very excited when you use a high-pitched playful voice and make "ch-ch" or "ts-ts" tongue sounds. Following are some common games rat owners enjoy with their pets:

Rats love to play games.

Get the Rat   This game is based on chasing and tickling. Rats of all ages will play this among themselves. This entails chasing the rat and then tickling or softly grabbing at him with "gotcha, gotcha" type exclamations. You then have your hand "run away" and when the rat follows, you turn and chase him again repeating the scenario. Most rats enjoy this game and get quite excited. They'll hop and leap while running to and fro, and when the game ends will try to draw you into continuing by chasing you and attacking your hand.

Wrestling   This is another action that rats do among themselves. Don't be too rough or your rat may follow suit and nip or scratch. When your rat is feeling comfortable with you, start poking and pushing him (gently!) and make excited sounds. Usually your rat will respond by grabbing at you and wrestling, like a cat who rolls around and kicks with her hind feet. If your

115

rat gets too excited and begins to get too rough, say "No!" in a firm voice and stop the game. Speak gently to him and pet him softly, but put off the game for another time. This game works well in combination with Get the Rat since wrestling is tiring and switching to a different game will give your rat a break.

Peek-a-boo   Most rats enjoy a good game of peek-a-boo. They naturally hide during their playtimes and will peek out at you periodically. If you spot them, you can say "see you" in a playful voice and point or reach for them. They will dart back and peek out again, sometimes from the same place and sometimes from a hiding place across the room.

Hide-and-seek   Play hide-and-seek with your rat's favorite toy. Some rats will play hide-and-seek with a toy that is easy to carry, like a bird toy. Show the rat you are playing with his toy and act like you are enjoying yourself, then hide it behind your back or in the couch. Your rat will go look for it, but be forewarned, he won't always bring you what he retrieves. Sometimes this game only works once and then he takes his treasure to a different spot and squirrels it away.

TRICKS

Tricks are different from games. A trick is a controlled behavior, whereas a game is more like free play. Rats respond well to training and perform easily. Your first course of action is to determine what treats your rat dearly loves. Pick something small and light since you may be giving a lot of them over a short time period. Cereals are a good choice. Decide what trick you are going to focus on. It is best to start with an easy one that is close to something your rat does naturally. Once your rat masters one trick, the other ones are much easier.

Rats respond best to positive reinforcement and not punishment. If you feel you must punish your rat for offenses, never strike him, but use the time-out method and put him back in his cage and don't give him any attention for a few minutes. This can have a great impact.

There are several possible tricks you can teach your rat. Anything that resembles a rat behavior can most likely be turned into a trick—all you need is patience and a willing rat. Not all rats will respond to training. Some are harder to work with than others and some just want to play. Basic rat tricks include the following:

Come This is the basic "come here" that people teach their dogs. If you'd like to teach your ratty to come to you when you call him, you need to establish his name in his mind. Use it as often as you can when talking to him. Soon, he will realize that the name you say pertains to him and will respond to it. When you decide to work on the come command, let your rat have some playtime and then break out the special treat. Show it to your rat and say your rat's name and "Come." Hold the treat just out of his reach and encourage him again to come and take the treat. If he takes a few steps toward you, praise him and give him the treat. Do this several times and then start moving the treat farther away and make him walk farther to get it. Once he has the idea, he will anticipate the treat and come quickly when you call him. You will find that if your rat really likes the treat, you can call him and he will fly out of wherever he is and land on your lap for his treat.

Riding on Your Shoulder For some rats this comes naturally, but for others it is a chore. If you'd like to teach your rat to sit on your shoulder, try short intervals at first to gauge your rat's reaction. If he doesn't seem to mind and just sits, he may be a natural shoulder rat. If, however, he looks about and decides that's all there is to see, he will begin climbing down your front or back looking for more excitement. Put him back on your shoulder and talk to him quietly. Praise

---

TRAINING YOUR RAT

Below are some guidelines for training your rat to do tricks:

- Work with your rat on several short training sessions instead of one long one.

- Try to work with your rat at the same time each day.

- Let your rat have some playtime first to release excess energy.

- Be consistent with your requests.

- Reserve whatever treat you've chosen only for training.

- Always start with the treat for the reward, then try to substitute praise and affection for some of the milestones.

- Rats, like dogs, respond to single word phrases best.

him for being on your shoulder and then give him a treat. When he's finished with the treat, just as you start to lose his attention, praise him again and give him a break. With this type of trick, you want to do it slowly and give frequent breaks. Otherwise, a rat's busybody-ness will cause him to become frustrated and he may get rambunctious. It is best to do it slowly and let your rat learn the rewards for coop-eration. Gradually increase the time and intervals on your shoulder. When you feel your rat is comfortable for a few minutes, try walking around the house a bit and make sure he stays there. Rats adapt easily to the balancing and begin to enjoy seeing the sights.

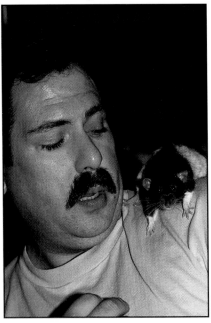

Some rats easily master staying on your shoulder, but for other rats it can be a challenge!

Riding in a Pack   Some peo-ple prefer to have their rat in a pack-type carrier. There are commercial pet packs or you may use a simple bag or fanny pack. The same rules from above apply. Train your rat in short and frequent intervals. Do not zip or close your pack. This could frighten your rat and could also limit his oxygen. Also, tails seem to get caught easily in those zippers. Reassure your rat that this is exactly what you would like and that he is perfectly safe. Eventually, as with riding on the shoulder, your rat will usually adapt to riding in a pack.

Sit-up   This is a rat behavior that is easily adapted to a trick. Rats can stand on their hind legs with little effort. For this, you would use the same method as you would with a dog. Using the rat's name, tell him to sit-up and hold a treat over his head. When he stands up, praise him and give him the treat. In each session, encourage him to stand a bit longer than before. Eventually, he will sit up on command or when you sweep your finger up toward the ceiling.

Going Through a Hoop You can teach your rat to go through a hoop with a little hop. Start by getting a hoop big enough for your rat to fit comfortably through. Put the hoop vertically on the ground and hold a treat on the other side. Call your rat and encourage him to go through the hoop. When he steps through the hoop, praise him and give him a treat. When he is adept at this, raise the hoop off the ground ¼ inch and encourage him to go through it. Keep raising the hoop until it is at a level where your rat does a little hop.

Playing Ball Rats love to play ball, and any trick that utilizes a ball will become a favorite. First, you must teach the rat that the ball is yours. Rats will often take the ball to their stash as their own treasure. You must tell them no and retrieve it. Start with a simple ball behavior such as "catch," where you roll the ball to your rat and he brings it to you. After you roll the ball to your rat, call him by name and tell him to come. If your rat takes even a step, praise him and give him a treat. Keep doing this until he will return the ball to you. After this is accomplished, you can try soccer or basketball. Each game is essentially the same as "catch" except you want the rat to put the ball somewhere else. With soccer, you want him to bat the ball with his paws or feet to a designated spot. Remember to start with small goals and work to larger ones. Praise your rat often and give treats. With basketball, your rat will pick up the ball as in "catch" and put it in a basket or designated area. When beginning, encourage your rat to carry the ball to the designated spot instead of to you. Praise him and give treats when he goes in the right direction. Work with small steps and soon you will have a very impressive trickster to amaze your family and friends.

> ### BE PATIENT
>
> Remember with all training, if you are patient, consistent and positive, you can accomplish great things. Rats enjoy learning and pleasing you. Different rats have different personalities, and this may affect the rate and extent of their learning, but they can all be taught some basic skills. Spending time teaching them not only results in neat things to show and a great sense of accomplishment, but it helps you spend quality time with your rat. Your rat will come to enjoy these sessions and look forward to learning from you.

chapter 10

Showing
Your Rat

It is a common human trait to want to show your pet, and rat owners are no exception. We all want to show off our pets because we think they are the best and most beautiful. There are several clubs that hold shows, and you may live close enough to one to participate.

Show Quality

Is your rat show quality or pet quality? If she isn't show quality, she can still be shown in the pet class and obtain a ribbon or sometimes a trophy. Consult chapter 3 for an over-view on rat varieties. If you feel that your rat resembles one of the accepted descriptions, talk to the show sec-retary or a club member to verify your entry. Although most judges will set aside an animal entered incorrectly to be put in the right class, if the class has already been shown, your rat will be dis-qualified. This can be very disap-pointing.

Preparing Your Rat for the Show

Rats, thankfully, don't need much preparation for shows. You will need to prepare a transportation carrier for her. This can be her own cage if it is portable enough and you are comfortable carrying it. There are several carriers avail-able on the market that work well. Make sure you have clean bedding in the carrier, plus some extra in case of accidents; plenty of extra water; your rat's water bottle (don't put it in the cage while traveling as it will leak); extra food; healthy snacks like fruits or veggies; and warm items (box or blankies) if it's cold or cold packs (frozen water) if it's warm.

A TYPICAL JUDGING SYSTEM

Below is a sample of a judge's point system:

Color, Marking and Variety	50	points
Temperament	15	points
Type	5	points
Condition	5	points
Head	5	points
Eyes	5	points
Ears	5	points
Tail	5	points
Size	5	points
TOTAL	100	points

The judge comments on each attribute of the rat in comparison to the Standards of Perfection. The rat in each class who best resem-bles the standard places first.

part four

Beyond
the
Basics

chapter 11

Recommended Reading

Books on rats for pet owners are not plentiful at this point. There are many books on the scientific aspects of rats available in libraries. The following is a list of books that may be helpful to you, the pet owner.

Bailey, Jill. *Discovering Rats and Mice*. Neshkora, WI: Bookwright, 1987.

Fox, Susan. *Rats*. Neptune City, NJ: T.F.H. Publications, 1988.

Himsel, Carol A. *Rats*. Hauppauge, NY: Barron's Educational Series, Inc. 1991.

Mays, Nick. *The Proper Care of Fancy Rats*. Neptune City, NJ: T.F.H. Publications, 1993.

For other publications, it is advisable to contact rat and mouse clubs; they may have pamphlets and booklets for sale on various subjects. Other sources are humane societies, local animal shelters or rescue groups, college biology departments, cage manufacturers and feed stores.

A Word About the Internet

If you have access to the Internet, there are wonderful Web sites with lots of information. Due to the transient nature of Web sites and e-mail addresses, I have chosen not to list any here for they can be out of date very quickly. You can, however, use search engines to name your criteria and be able to view scientific data, genetics information, club information and people's personal pages with photos and discussions about their rats.

chapter 12

Resources

Below is a current list of known clubs that hold regular meetings and/or shows. Many of the clubs have Web sites on-line, so if you have Internet access, you can look them up and read more about them.

American Fancy Rat & Mouse Association (AFRMA)
9230 64th St.
Riverside, CA 92509-5924

American Rat, Mouse & Hamster Society (ARMHS)
P.O. Box 1451
Ramona, CA 92065

Midwest Rat and Mouse Club
7409 Cimmaron Station
Columbus, OH 43235

Michigan Rat Fanciers
21½ Dennis SE
Grand Rapids, MI 49506

National Fancy Rat Society (NFRS)
14 Clayhill House
Somers Close, Reigate
Surrey, RH2 9EB
England

Northeast Rat & Mouse Club International (NRMCI)
603 Brandt Ave.
New Cumberland, PA 17070

Pacific Northwest Pet and Show Rat Club
423 E. Harrison
Tacoma, WA 98404

Rat Fan Club (RFC)
857 Lindo Lane
Chico, CA 95926

Rat & Mouse Club of America (RMCA)—Home Chapter
13075 Springdale St., Suite 302
Westminister, CA 92683

Rat & Mouse Club of America (RMCA)—Colorado Chapter
P.O. Box 62655
Colorado Springs, CO 80962-2655

Rat & Mouse Club of America (RMCA)—San Francisco Chapter
2901 College Ave. #107
Livermore, CA 94550
or
484 15th Ave.
Menlo Park, CA 94025

Rat, Mouse & Hamster Fanciers (RMHF)
188 School St.
Danville, CA 94526

Rat Rescue

Some of the clubs, such as the RMCA, offer rescue services for unwanted animals. If you are interested in a rescue situation, please contact the nearest club to see if they have a rescue section set up.